STREET FOOD COOKBOOK

NORTHERN EDITION

The Street Food Cook Book

©2015 Meze Publishing.
All rights reserved.

First edition printed in 2015 in the UK.
ISBN: 978-1-910863-06-0

Compiled by: Amanda Perry, Phil Turner

Written by: Kate Eddison

Photography by: Tim Green
www.timgreenphotographer.co.uk

Marc Barker
www.marcabarker.com

Edited by: Kerre Chen

Designed by: Paul Cocker, Marc Barker

Contributors: Kelsie Marsden, Faye Bailey

me:ze
PUBLISHING

Published by Meze Publishing Limited
Unit 1 Beehive Works
Milton Street
Sheffield S3 7WL
Web: www.mezepublishing.co.uk
Tel: 0114 275 7709
Email: info@mezepublishing.co.uk

CONTENTS

INTRODUCTION –
A STREET FOOD REVOLUTION 6

STREETZINE – THE NORTH'S
BEST STREET FOOD AND WHERE TO FIND IT 8

BUDDHA BELLY 14
GRILLED CHICKEN AND STICKY RICE
WITH PAPAYA SALAD (SOM TAM) 16

SMOKIN' BLUES 20
BEEF SHORT RIBS
AND SWEET PICKLED SHALLOTS 22
MOINK BALLS AND SLAW 24

THE HOG STOP 28
PORCHETTA SAUCE 30

STREET FOOD CHEF 34
CHICKEN MOLE AND SALSA VERDE 36

SUNSHINE PIZZA OVEN 40
CLASSIC MARGHERITA PIZZA 42

CRÊPE LUCETTE 46
BANOFFEE CRÊPES 48
GENTLEMAN'S BRUNCH 50

PIE EYED 54
BEEF BRISKET, BLACK SHEEP ALE
AND CHILLI CHORIZO JAM 56

PIZZETTE 60
PIZZA CINGHIALE 62

FANCY AN INDIAN 66
PILCHARD CURRY 68

PERCY & LILY'S 72
ARGENTINIAN CHORIPÁN 74
LEBANESE FLATBREAD 76

KITSCH'N CRÊPE CO. 80
STRAWBERRY SUNDAE CRÊPES
WITH CHOCOLATE GANACHE FILLING 82

GINGER BAKERS 86
CHOCOLATE NANCY 88

KHOO'S HOT SAUCE 92
KHOO'S JERK CHICKEN 94

LIBERTY FOODS 96
CURRIED SCOTCH EGGS 96

MAGPIE CAFÉ STREET FOOD 100
CRISPY COD BAP WITH SPICY
SEAFOOD SAUCE 102

PIZZA LOCO 106
SHREDDED DUCK WITH HERB-INFUSED
HONEY, BALSAMIC FIGS & BRIE 108
PANCETTA, PICKLED DAMSONS
AND CREAMY GOATS CURD PIZZA 110

SMO•FO SMOKED FOOD 112
PINT OF HICKORY SMOKED
PORK SCRATCHINGS 112

CAFE CEREZA 116

BOSTON SHAKERS 122
COCKTAIL SELECTION 124

INTRODUCTION
A STREET FOOD REVOLUTION

A relatively new concept in the UK, street food comes in all shapes and sizes – hot or cold, quick-cooked or slowly simmered, wrapped or rolled, sweet or savoury… what ties it together is the passion that is shared by the artisan traders who bring gourmet dishes out from restaurants and onto the streets.

It's thought that the term 'street food' came from the American tradition of street food trucks, and it goes without saying that many of the best British traders have captured the tastes and traditions of those American classics – top-quality meat cooked low and slow until it falls apart (think pulled pork, succulent ribs or beef brisket), juicy burgers made using the very finest meat or hotdogs piled high with a mind-boggling array of toppings.

However, street food is eaten all over the world, historically being the affordable option for people on their way to work or grabbing a quick snack. From dosas and banh mi to pizza slices and galettes, inspiration from all over the globe is found in the wafting aromas, sizzling sounds and fiery flavours that engulf the senses at any British street food market.

The Northern cities are at the forefront of this exciting culinary trend. Ambitious and passionate foodies have brought local ingredients and top-quality cooking to the streets, creating amazing flavour combinations in front of our eyes and dishing them up at affordable prices. From Birmingham to Newcastle, there are so many markets and vendors, you could spend a year trying them all. Nottingham, Loughborough, Sheffield, Hull, Leeds, Manchester, Darlington and Sunderland all have incredible traders putting them firmly on the street food map, but there is also plenty going on outside the major cities.

Whether you're in the Lake District, North Yorkshire or the Peak District, you'll find inspiration in this book for incredible food to try. You'll also find those talented artisan vendors who can create delicious menus for your party, wedding or special event. Whether it's being served up from a tent, van or mobile pizza oven – if it's made on the move, it's covered in this book.

THE NORTH'S BEST STREET FOOD AND WHERE TO FIND IT

THE RISE AND POPULARITY OF STREET FOOD OVER RECENT YEARS HAS SEEN A HUGE NATIONWIDE INCREASE OF SPECIALISED FOODIE EVENTS, SHOWCASING SOME OF THE FINEST VENDORS AROUND. STREETZINE, THE UK'S ONLINE STREET FOOD MAGAZINE PICK SOME OF THE FINEST...

The relentless time and effort that street food vendors spend perfecting their dishes knows no bounds. Creating diverse and highly innovative street food is pure labour of love and the end results wouldn't look or feel out of place in many high-end restaurants, yet it's done at a fraction of the cost with no pomp and ceremony – just great food and theatre.

So where can I find and eat these wonderful creations? Here's our guide (in no particular order) to some of the best places to eat street food in the North – enjoy!

THE EBOR FEAST – YORK

The aim of the Ebor Feast organisers is simple: to gather together the best independent street food traders, craft brewers and artisan distillers, and to create bespoke events in the beautiful city of York.

Check out regulars like The Mussel Pot, who serve the best fresh-cooked mussels this side of Normandy. Or if it's gourmet kebabs you're after, then no visit to The Ebor Feast would be complete without popping by Shambles Kitchen. If you crave American BBQ done right, using Yorkshire's finest produce, then visit regulars, Smokin Blues (featured on page 20) and try their smoked beef rib sandwich, probably the best we've ever tasted!

@FeastinYork

GREAT TASTE FESTIVAL OF FOOD & DRINK CLUMBER PARK, NOTTS

Now in its third year, the Great Taste Festival is set in the heart of The National Trust's beautiful Clumber Park. Here you will find a diverse range of world street food to tempt your taste buds whilst browsing the artisan food producer stalls or perhaps watching John Torode entertain the crowd with his cooking demonstrations. Be sure to swing by the Pizza Peddlers, who serve delicious authentic wood-fired Pizza from 'Rowlie', a beautifully converted vintage Citroen H Van.

www.festivaloffoodanddrink.co.uk

LEVY MARKET LEVENSHULME, MANCHESTER

Levy Market prides itself on its diverse range of high-quality traders. At every market you can expect an ever-changing line-up of 50 artisan traders selling street food and produce, as well as plants, gifts, vintage clothing and homeware.

www.levymarket.com

B.EAT STREET – MANCHESTER

With its proposed three bars, six micro-diners and covered year round terrace, this is where some of Manchester's finest street food vendors will gather to unleash street food of outstanding quality and variety. Personal favourites and past B.eat Street regulars are Dirty Food Revolution, self-proclaimed extreme 'foodamentalists', specialising in dirty mile-high street food burgers.

www.beatstreetmcr.co.uk

BRUM YUM YUM – KING'S HEATH, BIRMINGHAM

More Midlands than North, but we feel Brum Yum Yum is well worth a diversion further south! The most honest and lovingly prepared food you'll eat anywhere outside your grandma's kitchen. No restaurant can match it, because what you see really is what you get. And if you want to know more, just ask as you watch it being prepared; Brum Yum Yum street food vendors know where every ingredient comes from. They probably raised those porkers themselves, but if not, they will no doubt tell you the name of the farm where each little piggy came from.

www.brumyumyum.co.uk

GRILLSTOCK – ALBERT SQUARE, MANCHESTER

Grillstock Manchester offers festival-goers an authentic Southern US barbecue experience. Once a year, thousands of hungry party-goers descend on Albert Square to enjoy a weekend of proper Southern-style hospitality with heaps of meat, music and mayhem thrown in for pure indulgence!

Awesome DJs, top bands, craft beers and incredible food are all in abundance at Grillstock Manchester, which saw McSlims BBQ take away the deserved 2015 Grand Champion trophy with Reserve Grand Champion going to Bunch of Swines and the coveted Dr.BBQ Award going to Flamin' Amateurs.

Watch some headline bands play on the main stage and try Lola's Wings, preferably smothered in Frank's RedHot Sauce, or savour the delights from BBQ masters The Churrasco Gang, whose mouth-watering Brazilian beef and chicken, cooked over hot coals on an amazing rotisserie machine, is one definitely not to be missed!

www.grillstock.co.uk/manchester-festival

There are many more great street food events of course, too many to list here, but you can find them all by visiting: www.streetfoodnews.co.uk/events

BUDDHA BELLY

FOR A TASTE OF THE REAL THAILAND, YOU NO LONGER NEED TO GET OFF THE BEATEN TRACK AND VISIT RURAL THAI VILLAGES, AS BUDDHA BELLY HAS BROUGHT AUTHENTIC RECIPES TO THE BRITISH STREETS.

The Buddha Belly story began in 1967 when Sai Deethwa's mother Niang learnt from her own mother how to prepare the family recipes for their local market in Surin, Thailand. By the age of six, Niang was preparing the secret family Thai green curry recipe along with the other dishes that would become the foundation for feeding her own family in years to come.

Sai's mother was 23 when she moved to the UK with three-year-old Sai. Soon, the people of Gloucester were tucking into Niang's authentic Thai dishes and Sai grew up inspired by her mother's ability to turn the most unusual ingredients into incredible meals. Sai immersed herself in cookbooks, developed a love of foraging for fresh ingredients and grew to be passionate about all things food.

When Sai became one of the 24 people selected for Masterchef UK in 2012 out of 20,000 applicants, she was encouraged to begin her career in the food industry with her partner James. It's safe to say this ambitious pair have never looked back. With recognition stacking up within the industry – a Young British Foodies finalist in 2014 and winner of Midlands British Street Food Award and Best Street Food England and Wales at The Food Awards 2014 – Buddha Belly is now wowing crowds with authentic Thai cooking at markets across the UK.

The focus on quality ingredients is what truly shines in Buddha Belly's creations. The meat is all free-range and comes from James' dad, who has been a butcher for over 50 years, and everything is made completely from scratch, including their famous sweet and sour sauce. With such devotion to authentic cooking and generations of culinary secrets up her sleeve, it's no surprise that Sai's cooking really packs a flavourful punch – one thing is for sure, you won't taste Thai food like this anywhere else in the UK.

BUDDHA BELLY — PLEASE ASK ABOUT ALLERGENS!

Chicken, Chilli & Limeleaf Curry
fragrant & spicy Thai curry with Jasmine rice
(GLUTEN FREE with rice)
SPICY! £6

Marinated Crispy Chicken
Served with Spiced Veg Noodles
(DAIRY FREE)
£6

Vegan Yellow Thai Curry
Served with Jasmine rice (GLUTEN FREE)
(DAIRY FREE) £5.50

Lightly Spiced Veg Noodles (VEGAN) £4.50

Masterchef Contestant 2012
Winners & Best STREET FOOD
ENGLAND & WALES 2014
@saibuddhabelly

MADE IN THAILAND

BUDDHA BELLY

GRILLED CHICKEN & STICKY RICE WITH PAPAYA SALAD (SOM TAM)

THE PAPAYA SALAD IS ALWAYS MADE IN A PESTLE AND MORTAR OR "POK POK" AS IT'S COMMONLY KNOWN IN THAILAND DUE TO THE NOISE IT MAKES WHEN YOU'RE USING IT. PREPARE THE CARROT AND PAPAYA BY PEELING AND SHREDDING INTO LONG THIN STRANDS. THAIS NOW USE A PEELER SPECIFICALLY DESIGNED TO SHRED VEGETABLES IN THIS WAY. IF YOU CAN'T GET HOLD OF ONE OF THESE, A JULIENNE SHREDDER WILL WORK, BUT THE STRANDS MAY NOT BE AS FINE. FAILING THAT, YOU CAN DO THIS THE OLD FASHIONED WAY. TAKE THE PAPAYA AND REPEATEDLY STRIKE THE FLESH GENTLY WITH A MEAT CLEAVER UNTIL LONG STANDS COME AWAY FROM IT. A LABOUR OF LOVE! THE GLUTINOUS RICE NEEDS TO BE SOAKED FOR AT LEAST 4 HOURS BEFORE YOU STEAM IT, SO MAKE SURE YOU DO THIS WELL IN ADVANCE. SERVES 2.

FOR THE GRILLED CHICKEN:

1 tsp sugar

1 tsp salt

½ tsp fine white pepper

2 tbsp rapeseed oil

2 chicken legs, including thighs

FOR THE PAPAYA SALAD:

2 cloves garlic

2-6 red birds eye chillies

25g snake beans or fine beans

5 cherry tomatoes, halved

1 tbsp soy sauce

2 tbsp fish sauce

1-2 tsp sugar

Juice of 1 lemon

150g green papaya, peeled and shredded

50g carrot, peeled and shredded

FOR THE STICKY RICE:

400g Thai glutinous rice, soaked for at least 4 hours

For the grilled chicken, combine the sugar, salt, pepper and oil. Score the chicken legs to the bone and rub in the marinade. Grill on a medium heat for 10 minutes on each side until completely cooked. Allow to rest for 10 minutes before serving.

For the papaya salad, use a pestle and mortar to pound the garlic and chillies into a paste. Add the snake/fine beans and bruise them, but be careful not to pound them to a pulp. By bruising the beans, it allows them to soak up the flavour, but also still have some crunch. Add the halved tomatoes and again just bruise the tomatoes. Add the soy sauce, fish sauce, sugar and lemon juice. Combine and add more sugar or soy/fish sauce to your individual taste. Once you're happy, add the papaya and carrot and use a spoon along with the pestle to mix the som tam up. Watch out, it spits!

The glutinous rice must be steamed. Traditionally, a steel pot with a bamboo basket is used. If you don't have one of these, a normal steamer which sits on your hob works well. If steaming the rice in this way, you will need to either fill a muslin cloth with the sticky rice or use a metal mesh strainer. Steam the rice for 10 minutes. The rice will then need to be turned or flipped and then steamed again for another 10 minutes. This ensures that the rice has completely cooked.

Serve the sticky rice at once with the grilled chicken and the papaya salad or som tam. Thais love to eat som tam with some crunchy raw veg on the side.

SMOKIN' BLUES

SMOKIN' BLUES ARE BRINGING THE RELAXED VIBES OF THE SOUTHERN STATES OF AMERICA TO THE STREETS OF YORKSHIRE. IT'S TIME TO CELEBRATE THE SIMPLICITY OF MEAT, SMOKE AND MIND-BLOWING FLAVOURS.

Just a few years ago, Morgan and Kate had been living and working the fast-paced London lifestyle – Kate in The City and Morgan as a fine-dining chef – until they made the brave decision to cut loose from the long hours and hectic schedules that dominated their day-to-day lives. Soon, they embarked on a life-changing adventure around the world together; an adventure that would change their perspectives and shape their future.

They planned the journey around their common interest – food – and plotted a food-lover's map around the globe, ear-marking those places that were home to their favourite cuisines. They spent a lot of their time in the southern states of America, allured initially by its incredible flavours and then captivated by the whole culinary heritage they encountered there.

Huge hunks of meat were cooked low and slow for hours over burning wood, ready to be enjoyed at relaxed gatherings where music played and people savoured food that was so simple yet so unbelievably delicious. So far removed from the lives they'd left

behind, Kate and Morgan were filled with inspiration for this way of living and eating.

On their return, they set about their business plan with gusto. The ambition: to bring flavour-packed, Memphis-inspired food to the people of Yorkshire, using the finest British produce. This wasn't a plan that was hatched half-heartedly –the smoker was imported from America and the silver Airstream trailer was custom-built to house it. The idea was that they could make their smoker truly portable, so that they could always provide the freshest meat and the best flavour at every event.

Although the inspiration is whole-heartedly American, the ingredients are sourced from as close to home as possible from within Yorkshire. Morgan's homemade spice rubs and sauces are the result of years of development, endless taste-testing and tweaking.

For Smokin' Blues, if something is worth doing, it's worth doing properly. You'll be hard-pressed to find a more authentic taste of Tennessee on this side of the Atlantic.

SMOKEHOUSE
—∞— SPECIALS —∞—

SLIDERS 3 MINI BRIOCHE BUNS
£7
ONE OF EACH SMOKED MEATS:
1. BEEF RIB 2. PORK BELLY 3. CAJUN CHICKEN
WITH HOME MADE SAUCES + PICKLES

CHEEKY CHIPS £6.50
SMOKED & BRAISED OX CHEEKS
ON DOUBLE COOKED FRIES
WITH CRISPY SHALLOT RINGS

SMOKIN' BLUES
SMOKEHOUSE & BBQ

SMOKIN' BLUES
BEEF SHORT RIBS & SWEET PICKLED SHALLOTS

FOR THIS RECIPE WE WOULD RECOMMEND USING A HOME SMOKER. HOWEVER, THERE ARE WAYS OF PRODUCING THE SAME RESULTS WITH A CONVENTIONAL OVEN OR GAS BARBECUE GRILL. A BRIEF ONLINE SEARCH WILL EXPLAIN HOW.

PERFECT FOR MEAT LOVERS, THIS TAKE ON THE ICONIC TEXAS BARBECUE SPECIAL PACKS A HEFTY, FLAVOURSOME PUNCH WITH ONE RIB PER PERSON MAKING FOR AN AMPLE PORTION. FOR BEST RESULTS PREPARE THE PICKLED SHALLOTS A DAY IN ADVANCE. SERVES 6

FOR THE RIBS:

6 beef short ribs

Barbecue sauce, to serve

Bread bun, to serve (optional)

FOR THE DRY RUB:

200g coarse ground black pepper

50g brown sugar

100g salt

10g dried thyme

25g garlic powder

FOR THE SWEET PICKLED SHALLOTS:

500ml white wine vinegar

350g white sugar

100ml water

6 peppercorns

1 star anise

12 mustard seeds

2 cloves garlic

A few sprigs of thyme

500g shallots

First combine all the ingredients for the dry rub in a bowl and mix well. Apply a heavy coating to the ribs and leave in the fridge for 3-4 hours to marinate.

For the pickling liquid, put the vinegar, sugar, water, peppercorns, star anise, mustard seeds, garlic and thyme in a pan, bring to the boil and cook until the sugar is dissolved. Set aside and leave to cool. Pour the liquid through a sieve to remove the spices. Take the shallots and slice into thin rings, separating as much as possible. Add to the cooled liquid and leave to pickle (try to make these 1 day in advance).

Preheat the smoker to 105°C and place the beef ribs inside. Try using hickory or oak as these strong flavoured woods work really well with the beef. Cooking should take 8-10 hours depending on the size of the ribs; the internal temperature should reach 93°C. When done, remove and wrap in foil.

Serve 'Flintstone-style' (on the bone) with a few pickled shallots on top and your favourite barbecue sauce. Alternately take off the bone and dice into pieces, serving in a bread bun with pickles and barbecue sauce.

SMOKIN' BLUES

MOINK BALLS & SLAW

FOR THIS RECIPE WE WOULD RECOMMEND USING A HOME SMOKER. HOWEVER, THERE ARE WAYS OF PRODUCING THE SAME RESULTS WITH A CONVENTIONAL OVEN OR GAS BARBECUE GRILL. A BRIEF ONLINE SEARCH WILL EXPLAIN HOW.

MOINK BALLS, A COMBINATION OF BEEF (MOO) AND PORK (OINK), ARE A WINNING MEATY COMBINATION REVERED BY BARBECUE BUFFS IN THE USA.

MAKES 16

FOR THE BALLS:

500g beef mince

60g breadcrumbs

2 eggs

1 tbsp onion powder

1 tbsp garlic powder

1 tbsp dried oregano

½ tsp salt

½ tsp pepper

8 rashers smoked streaky bacon

Barbecue sauce, to glaze

FOR THE 'SLAW:

½ white cabbage

1/4 red cabbage

1 carrot

A small bunch of fresh coriander, chopped

30ml cider vinegar

3 tbsp mayonnaise

1 tsp paprika

Salt and black pepper

FOR THE RUB:

1 tbsp paprika

1 tbsp chilli powder

1 tsp salt

1 tsp black pepper

1 tsp brown sugar

1 tsp dried thyme

½ tsp cayenne pepper

Combine the mince, breadcrumbs, eggs, onion powder, garlic powder, oregano and seasoning in a bowl and mix well. Roll into 16 balls (about 40g each) and set aside. Next take the streaky bacon, cut the slices in half and roll around the meatballs using a toothpick to hold it in place.

For the 'slaw, slice the cabbages as thinly as possible. Peel and grate the carrot, add to a bowl with the cabbage and chopped coriander. Add the remaining ingredients to the mixture, season and mix well.

For the rub combine all the ingredients in a bowl and mix. Sprinkle the moink balls lightly with the rub and set aside.

Get your smoker to 105°C and place the moink balls inside. Leave to cook for 45 minutes. Remove the moink balls from the smoker and glaze with barbecue sauce. Return to the smoker for a further 20 minutes. When ready, remove from the smoker and serve with a side of 'slaw.

SLO
SOU

THE HOG STOP

THE GREAT BRITISH HOG ROAST HAS BEEN GIVEN AN
INTERNATIONAL TWIST IN LOUGHBOROUGH
WITH FLAVOURS FROM AROUND THE WORLD.
WELCOME TO THE HOG STOP.

The Hog Stop was set up in a fabulous converted bus shelter in the heart of vibrant Loughborough. Founder Paul is an established restaurateur and passionate food lover. Having already brought Mexican and Australian restaurants to Loughborough in The Cactus Café and Moomba, his next venture was inspired by trips to Italy, where food is firmly at the centre of life.

On his Italian travels, it was the porchetta trucks that caught Paul's attention. These trucks travel up and down the country selling slow-cooked pork from whole pigs, flavoured with rosemary, garlic, fennel and chilli. The pork is served in crusty ciabatta to be devoured by hungry locals at lunch time.

Back in Loughborough, Paul combined the idea of the porchetta truck with the classic British hog roast, and he has brought plenty of other flavours into the mix too. At The Hog Stop, the locally sourced, outdoor-bred pork is slow-cooked overnight in the specially imported ovens to achieve the utmost succulence and irresistible flavour.

The next day, you can choose how you want to enjoy it. Go for a traditional English roll with home-made apple sauce, sage and onion stuffing and crackling; Italian porchetta coated in garlic, fennel, chilli and rosemary sauce; American-style with home-made apple coleslaw and smokey barbecue sauce; Jamaican jerk with a fiery Scotch bonnet sauce and home-made banana chutney; or Chinese five-spice with hoisin sauce and Asian leaf salad. There is a selection of artisan rolls to choose from, and you can opt for 'the whole hog' (for a large portion) or 'the piglet' (for smaller appetites), as well as salad boxes, an all-day breakfast and even a BBQ beef brisket with horseradish slaw.

With The Hog Stop proving such a hit, the next step was the brand new trailer, which means that these delicious sarnies are now on the move, travelling around the region. You'll be able to spot The Hog Stop street food trailer in Loughborough Market Place and at various events, markets and festivals, and it's no surprise they are proving extremely popular at private parties and weddings, too.

SLOW ROASTED LOCALLY SOURCED PORK

THE WHOLE HOG

THE
HOG STOP
STREET FOOD

Slow roasted locally sourced pork in artisan rolls
www.thehogstop.co.uk

THE
HOG
STOP
STREET FOOD

Victor

HOG
STOP
STREET FOOD

THE HOG STOP
ROAST PORK & PORCHETTA SAUCE

AT THE HOG STOP OUR PORK SHOULDERS ARE COOKED OVERNIGHT AT 100°C FOR ABOUT 6 HOURS, WHICH PRODUCES SUCCULENT PORK WITH A MELT-IN-YOUR-MOUTH TEXTURE. IF YOU WANT SOME CRISPY CRACKLING, REMOVE THE SKIN ONCE THE PORK IS COOKED AND SEASON WITH A MIXTURE OF COARSE SEA SALT AND TABLE SALT, TURN THE OVEN UP TO 250°C AND ROAST THE SKIN UNTIL IT STARTS TO BLISTER. THE PORK CAN BE SERVED IN CRISPY CIABATTA ROLLS TOPPED WITH PORCHETTA SAUCE AND ROCKET OR, FOR AN ITALIAN STYLE SUNDAY LUNCH, WHY NOT SLICE THE COOKED PORK, SPOON OVER THE PORCHETTA SAUCE AND SERVE WITH ROASTED FENNEL AND CRISPY POTATOES. SERVES 20 ROLLS.

FOR THE SAUCE:

4 tbsp fennel seeds

15g rosemary, chopped

4 cloves garlic, chopped

30g flat leaf parsley, chopped

1 tbsp chilli flakes

2 tbsp lemon juice

1 tbsp brown sugar

1 tbsp coarse sea salt

150ml extra virgin olive oil

150ml water

1 tbsp Dijon mustard

TO SERVE:

Roast pork

Ciabatta rolls

Soak the fennel seeds in boiling water for 30 minutes, then rinse them under cold water in a sieve. Put the soaked fennel seeds and all the other ingredients into a bowl and blend using a hand blender or in a food processer to a thick sauce. It's as simple as that!

Spoon the sauce onto roast pork in fresh ciabatta rolls and enjoy.

STREET FOOD CHEF

ZINGY, SPICY, FRESH AND NUTRITIOUS – STREET FOOD CHEF PACK THEIR BURRITOS WITH ALL THE GOOD THINGS THAT KEEP THEIR CUSTOMERS COMING BACK FOR MORE.

For husband and wife team Richard and Abi, one thing they have always believed in is the amazing power of 'proper food' – we're simply talking wholesome ingredients, free from additives and freshly cooked. Abi's background in 'early years' had shown her first-hand what a difference it can make to everyday life when people are eating a balanced fresh meal.

With such passion for cooking, it came as no surprise to their family when Abi and Richard decided to leave their jobs in 2009 and turn their shared love of food into a business. The Sheffield street food scene was creating quite a buzz and there was no better time to join this vibrant foodie community. "Our business values are all about supporting other local businesses. The Sheffield business and food communities have just been so welcoming to us," says Abi.

Street Food Chef source all their meat locally, of course. The chicken and beef come from Yorkshire and the pork is sourced from Moss Valley Fine Meats. However, it's not just the ingredients that come from close to home; the packaging and t-shirts are printed locally, too.

Everything is made from scratch and dished up at their mobile kitchen on Pinstone Street in Sheffield, as well as the licenced canteen on Arundel Street, where customers can sit down and enjoy their food with a drink. Loyal customers, won over by the authentic spices and fresh flavours, love the theatre of this type of food – the experience here is a world away from buying a pre-packaged sandwich on your lunch break, that's for sure. Mexican cuisine lends itself to being made right in front of your eyes, leaving customers' mouths watering as they pick from the fresh ingredients in front of them.

And it isn't just the Sheffield burrito fans who are queuing up to praise Street Food Chef – they've collected an Eat Sheffield award every year since 2011, a Reader Recommendation in the Good Food Guide 2013 and a runner up award in the Observer Food Monthly Awards 2014 for Best Cheap Eats. This little Mexican kitchen is proving that fast food can be nutritious as well as utterly delicious.

STREET FOOD CHEF
CHICKEN MOLE AND SALSA VERDE

1 stick of celery

1 green chilli (optional)

1 clove garlic (optional)

4 chicken breasts

7g sesame seeds

Salt and black pepper

Rice, to serve

FOR THE MOLE SAUCE:

2 dried ancho chillies

2 dried pasilla chillies

2 dried mulato chillies

1 tsp oil

60g onion, diced

1 clove garlic

60g tomatoes, roasted/charred

80g tomatillos, roasted/charred

4 tsp sesame seeds

4 tsp almonds

2 tsp peanuts

1 tsp pumpkin seeds

1 tsp coriander seeds

1 tsp ground all-spice

2 cloves

1 star anise

2 tsp raisins

6 tortilla chips, broken up

Half a slice of stale/toasted white bread or baguette, chopped

1 cinnamon stick

1½ tsp sugar

650ml chicken stock

80g dark chocolate, 70% cocoa

Salt and black pepper

FOR THE SALSA VERDE:

15g garlic

15g green chillies

370g tomatillos

90g onion, finely chopped

90g jalapenos

½ a bunch of fresh coriander (leaves and stalks)

20ml lime juice

½ tsp salt

MOLE IS A TRADITIONAL MEXICAN SAUCE THAT IS SERVED OVER MEAT. WE MAKE OUR OWN MOLE POBLANO AND SERVE IT WITH CHICKEN, ALTHOUGH WE HAVE ALSO SERVED IT WITH BEEF BRISKET. SERVES 4.

MOLE SAUCE

Bring a pan of water to the boil, add the chillies and simmer for 20 minutes until soft. Drain and allow to cool. Remove the stems.

Heat the oil in a pan, add the onion and garlic and sauté for 2-3 minutes. Add the tomatoes and tomatillos and sauté for 2-3 minutes.

Meanwhile, in a separate dry frying pan, dry roast the sesame seeds, almonds, peanuts, pumpkin seeds, coriander seeds, all-spice, cloves and star anise, being careful not to let them burn. Add them to the tomato and onion mixture, adding in the raisins, tortillas, bread, cinnamon stick, sugar, a pinch of salt and pepper and the chicken stock and bring to the boil. Reduce the heat and simmer for 15 minutes. After this time, remove the pan from the heat and stir in the chocolate. Blitz in a food processor until smooth and allow to cool. The mole sauce will yield 1 litre and will keep in the fridge for 7 days or the freezer for 3 months. Freeze it in small (50ml) batches so you can just take out one portion at a time.

SALSA VERDE

Place the garlic, chillies, tomatillos, onion, jalapenos in blender and blitz. Add the coriander and pulse till smooth. Add the lime juice and salt to taste.

CHICKEN MOLE

Bring a pan of water to the boil, add salt, pepper and a stick of celery. Add a green chilli and a garlic clove, if you like. Season the chicken breasts, and poach them in the water for about 25 minutes or until cooked through. Remove the chicken, reserving the stock. Chop the chicken into bite-sized pieces.

Combine 50ml of the mole sauce with 20ml of the reserved chicken stock. Add the sesame seeds. Spoon over the chicken pieces and serve with rice and salsa verde. (Alternatively serve as tacos with iceberg lettuce, sour cream, chopped coriander, jalapenos and a squeeze of lime.)

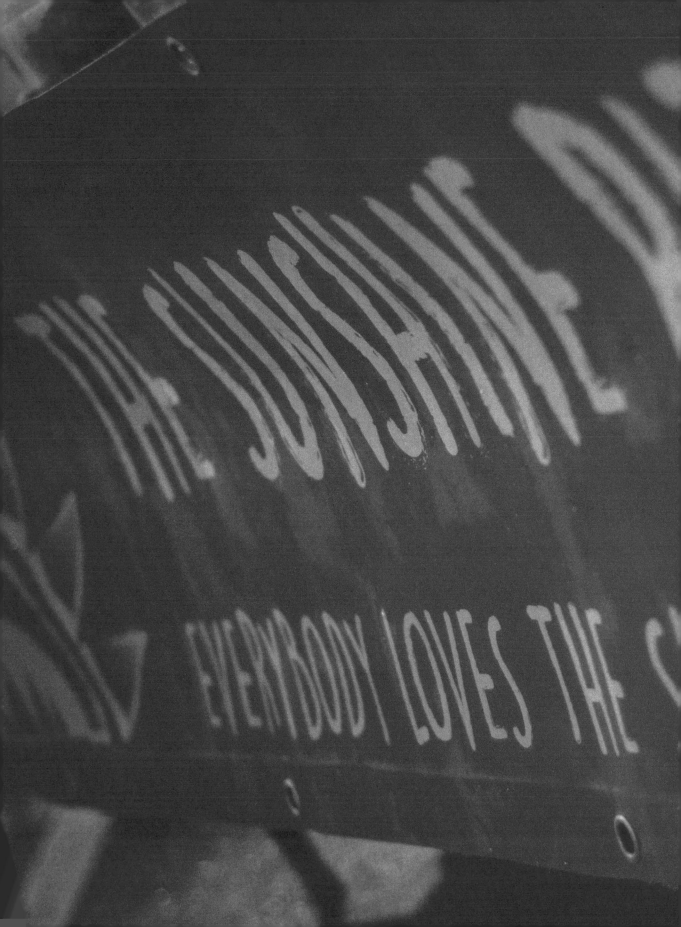

SUNSHINE PIZZA OVEN

SERVING UP HAND-MADE ARTISAN PIZZAS FROM THEIR SCENIC SPOT AT STANAGE EDGE OR AT EVENTS AROUND SHEFFIELD, YOU CAN RELY ON THE SUNSHINE PIZZA OVEN TO DELIVER A DOSE OF SUNSHINE WITH EACH AND EVERY SLICE.

Sarah Lagden and Dan Cox are the dough-licious dream team behind the success of The Sunshine Pizza Oven. They have been fuelling walkers, cyclists, climbers, tourists and locals with their heavenly stone-baked pizzas all summer at Stanage Edge. And, let's face it, Italian streets are all well and good, but there really is no better place to enjoy a hand-made pizza, fresh from the oven, than this stunning Peak District beauty spot.

The pizzas have proved such a hit here it's a good job the British-made oven can cook pizzas in around 90 seconds, which is thanks to its soaring temperature that reaches 450°C. Demonstrating their commitment to the environment, the oven is fuelled by local and sustainably sourced wood, and all the packaging is re-usable, recyclable or biodegradable.

Although the ethics are decidedly 'local', the pizzas certainly have that authentic Italian charm – the perfect combination for Sheffield pizza lovers! Sarah and Dan have chosen not to mess with the Italian classic too much, keeping things simple with traditional toppings of which Neapolitan pizza-makers would be proud, such as pepperoni, salami, olives, mozzarella, anchovies, tomatoes and basil.

The quality of the ingredients speaks for itself. Local and ethical suppliers are favoured and Sarah and Dan choose organic where possible. The dough is hand-made using organic stone-ground flour, salt, yeast and water, and dusted with semolina. Customers always comment on how easily digestible the bases are, but they also offer gluten-free bases for those who'd like to avoid gluten altogether and still enjoy a tasty pizza.

Vegans are always delighted to find that they have an option with vegan cheese, too.

With teas, coffees, cold drinks and a selection of home-made cakes also on offer, Sarah and Dan make sure that all their customers leave full and happy, whether they're off on the next step on their Peak District hike, visiting a community event or ready to dance the night away at a private party or wedding. For pizzas in Sheffield and Derbyshire, The Sunshine Pizza Oven really have got it all covered.

WOOD FIRED
PIZZA

GARLIC BREAD
MARGHERITA   £3.50
PESTO PIZZA
ITALIAN   £5.00
VEGGIE FULL H
NEAPOLITAN   £5.00

SUNSHINE PIZZA COMPANY

CLASSIC MARGHERITA PIZZA

WE USE GILCHESTER ORGANIC PIZZA AND CIABATTA FLOUR IN OUR DOUGH, WHICH IS A STONEGROUND RARE BRITISH WHEAT KNOWN FOR BEING PURE AND EASILY DIGESTIBLE. MAKES 6-8

FOR THE DOUGH:

1kg flour

640ml water

1g yeast

15g salt

FOR THE SAUCE:

2 tins of tomatoes

2 red onions, finely chopped

2-3 cloves garlic, finely chopped

1 tbsp dried oregano

Olive oil

Salt and pepper

Fresh basil leaves

Sliced fresh mozzarella

Semolina, for dusting

Toppings of your choice

For the dough, mix the flour and water together and then leave to stand for 20 minutes. Mix the yeast with a quarter of a cup of lukewarm water and allow to froth. Add the yeast mixture to the flour mixture along with the salt. Bring together into a dough and then knead until smooth. Cover and allow to prove for 1 hour until doubled in size.

Knead the dough briefly and then portion it into 6-8 dough balls. Dust them in flour and store them in sandwich bags in the fridge for up to 2 days (or in the freezer for up to 1 week).

For the sauce, drain the tomatoes and put the juice in a pan. Reduce the juice by half, then add the tomatoes. In a separate pan, sweat the onions and garlic in olive oil until softened. Add the softened onions to the tomatoes, along with the oregano and season with salt and pepper. Simmer until you have a sauce consistency. You can freeze the sauce, if you like.

When ready to cook, preheat the oven to as hot as the oven goes. To shape the dough balls, dust them with semolina and use the palm of your hand to flatten the dough balls into rounds, pushing gently from the middle out to keep a ½-1cm crust around the edge. Aim for a diameter of about 10-12 inches.

Spread the sauce on the base and add the toppings of your choice. For a classic margherita place basil leaves covered by slices of mozzarella on top, followed by a sprinkling of oregano. Cook in the preheated oven until the base is crisp and the toppings are bubbling.

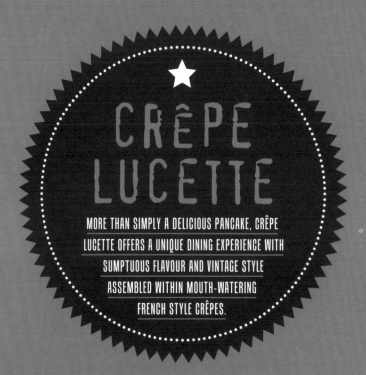

CRÊPE LUCETTE

MORE THAN SIMPLY A DELICIOUS PANCAKE, CRÊPE LUCETTE OFFERS A UNIQUE DINING EXPERIENCE WITH SUMPTUOUS FLAVOUR AND VINTAGE STYLE ASSEMBLED WITHIN MOUTH-WATERING FRENCH STYLE CRÊPES.

Flour, eggs, milk and a little je ne sais quois… there's something extraordinary about Crêpe Lucette. So what is it that makes these crêpes so special? Lucie Mountain trained in Brittany, the crêpe capital of the world, honing her crêpes to perfection and learning all the secrets of the traditional French crêperie. She brought her newly acquired skills back to Lincolnshire, along with those other vital Gallic ingredients – a touch of glamour, romance and elegance.

The crêpes are lovingly made using the freshest ingredients. The fresh eggs are all free-range from Lincolnshire chickens who roam in the fields at Primrose Valley farm. The flour, where possible, is from Mount Pleasant Windmill in Lincolnshire and made from 100% organic British wheat, putting local British products at the heart of these French classics. A 'Select Lincolnshire' member, Crêpe Lucette promotes the very best local producers, which not only supports the food community, but ensures the very best quality and taste too.

What makes Crêpe Lucette so special is the way they create an experience for all the senses – not just the taste buds. The Lucettes bring panache to any occasion, oozing glamour from their high heels

to their feathered fascinators. Vintage crockery, charming bunting and soft swing music complete the unique ambience.

Crêpe Lucette has been known to team up with local restaurants and quirky locations to present 'Crêpes by Candlelight', a unique crêpe pop-up dining experience. Candles softly flicker to the dulcet tones of 1940's songbirds, capturing the imagination of chic diners while they are seduced by the sumptuous aromas, as the Lucettes move elegantly from table to table with mouth-watering treats. It is an evening of fun and frolics with a selection of delectable and creative crêpes, colourful cocktails served from teapots and live music that transports you back to an era of simple enjoyment.

Crêpe Lucette are also out and about all over the region and the UK, bringing their inimitable style to food markets, vintage fairs, weddings and festivals. Wherever their delightful crêperie pops up, you can be sure that the lovely Lucettes will be brightening the occasion, polka dot dresses on and red lipstick perfectly applied, transporting people back to the 1940s with a few simple ingredients and a sprinkle of French magic.

CRÊPE LUCETTE

BANOFFEE CRÊPES

PSSST. WE HAVE A LITTLE SECRET TO SHARE... DID YOU KNOW THAT YOU SHOULD ALWAYS MIX BATTER ANTI-CLOCKWISE? HOWEVER, IF YOU ARE MAKING BATTER ON A STORMY DAY, YOUR BODY AND THE ATMOSPHERE CREATES A DIFFERENT ENERGY WHICH CAN AFFECT THE BATTER, SO YOU SHOULD ALWAYS MIX THE BATTER CLOCKWISE DURING THESE TIMES! SERVES 6.

FOR THE CRÊPES:

2 large free-range eggs

200g plain flour

500ml semi-skimmed milk

Butter, for frying

FOR THE FILLING:

200g granulated sugar

90g salted butter

120ml double cream

1 tsp sea salt

3 bananas, sliced

400g jar of Biscoff biscuit spread

Whipped cream

Pour the eggs, milk and flour into a mixing bowl or blender and put on low power for about 20 seconds or until the batter is smooth and lump-free. (Tip: The batter settles better when you blend it on a lower setting as it creates less air, making a much tastier batter. To ensure you have the perfect batter, push the side of the mixing bowl and count until the batter settles. For the perfect batter consistency, the batter should stop wobbling around 6-7 seconds.) Place the batter in the fridge for 30 minutes to settle and avoid breakage when cooking.

Whilst the batter rests in the fridge, start preparing the filling. To make the salted caramel, heat the granulated sugar in a medium saucepan over medium heat. Swirl the pan occasionally to prevent lumps from forming. Once melted, add the butter and stir until it is completed melted. It should take around 2-3 minutes for the butter and sugar to melt completely. (Tip: Always use a silicone or wooden spoon to stir the hot sugar and butter as it becomes very hot and may splash you when bubbling in the saucepan.)

Slowly pour in the double cream while stirring and then allow the sauce to boil for 1 minute. Remove from the heat and stir in the sea salt. You can add more or less salt depending on your preference. Allow to cool. (Tip: Once made, this salted caramel can be stored for up to 2 weeks in the fridge in an air tight container.)

Prepare the crêpes by heating a frying pan over a medium-high heat until hot. Coat the pan lightly with butter, then loosely wipe off with kitchen roll. Pour a ladleful of batter into the pan, tilting and rotating the pan until the batter has covered the surface. Loosen the sides with a spatula and once the underside has browned, flip the crêpe over and cook for about 1 minute. Transfer to a plate.

Spread the Biscoff biscuit spread over the top right hand section of the crêpe and place sliced banana on top. (Tip: Place the biscuit spread in a microwavable bowl and heat in the microwave for 15 seconds, so that it is easy to spread on the crêpe.) Drizzle the salted caramel over the ingredients on the right-hand side of the crêpe.

Fold the crepe in half from left to right, and then again from bottom to top, to make a triangle. Drizzle some more salted caramel over the top and create a finishing touch with some whipped cream. Voila!

CRÊPE LUCETTE

GENTLEMAN'S BRUNCH

OUR UNIQUE TWIST ON THE ENGLISH BREAKFAST, INSPIRED BY THE FAMOUS BRETAGNE CRÊPE, WHICH IS FIT FOR A GENTLEMAN, OH AND A LADY OF COURSE! SERVES 6.

FOR THE CRÊPES:

2 large free-range eggs

200g plain flour

500ml semi-skimmed milk

Butter, for frying

FOR THE FILLING:

6 rashers smoked back bacon

50g salted butter

250g chestnut mushrooms, finely chopped

6 large free-range eggs

500g mature cheddar cheese, grated (we recommend Lincolnshire Poacher)

3 vine tomatoes, finely chopped

Sea Salt and Cracked black pepper

Pour the eggs, milk and flour into a mixing bowl or blender and put on low power for about 20 seconds or until the batter is smooth and lump-free. (Tip: The batter settles better when you blend it on a lower setting as it creates less air, making a much tastier batter. To ensure you have the perfect batter, push the side of the mixing bowl and count until the batter settles. For the perfect batter consistency, the batter should stop wobbling around 6-7 seconds.) Place the batter in the fridge for 30 minutes to settle and avoids breakage when cooking.

Whilst the batter rests in the fridge, start preparing the filling. Cook the bacon under the grill on a medium heat for around 10 minutes, depending on how crispy you like your bacon cooked. Once the bacon is cooked, place it on kitchen roll to soak up any remaining fat, then chop it up into small pieces.

Preheat a pan over a medium heat on the hob and add the butter. Once the butter has melted, add the chopped mushrooms and cook for 2-3 minutes, stirring occasionally. Add salt and pepper.

Prepare the crêpes by heating a frying pan over a medium-high heat until hot. Coat the pan lightly with butter, then loosely wipe off with kitchen roll. Pour a ladleful of batter into the pan, tilting and rotating the pan until the batter has covered the surface.

Loosen the sides with a spatula and, once the underside has browned, flip the crêpe over and crack an egg in the middle of the crêpe. Spread the white of the egg over the crêpe so that it cooks quicker, leaving the yolk untouched in the middle.

Sprinkle a handful of cheese around the egg, like you would a pizza. Place a teaspoonful of finely chopped tomatoes in three small piles around the egg. Repeat this with the mushrooms and again with the finally chopped bacon.

Fold each of the four corners of the crêpe inwards to make an envelope, leaving the egg yolk on display in the middle of the crêpe.

PIE EYED

STREET FOOD ISN'T ALL ABOUT EXOTIC FLAVOURS. PIE EYED IS PUTTING BRITISH COOKING AT THE HEART OF THE STREET FOOD SCENE IN SHEFFIELD... LET'S HEAR IT FOR THE CLASSIC BRITISH PIE.

After Jack Norman graduated from Leeds University and returned to his home city of Sheffield, he was excited to find the independent street food scene alive and kicking in the Steel City. A food-lover, Jack began working in restaurants while exploring the markets and food events in his spare time. Although he'd always harboured fantasies of starting his own street food business, it wasn't until he lost his dad that Jack found himself inspired to give it a go and follow his dreams.

Jack spent weeks travelling around Italy, a country that certainly knows how to celebrate cooking. What inspired him was how the Italians would put so much effort into their classics – from the simplest pizzas served up for lunch to home-made pasta eaten meal after meal. So much pride for their country's culinary heritage was on display everywhere he looked and Jack was blown away by the never-ending passion for cooking their own timeless classics to perfection.

Back in Blighty, his thoughts turned to what he as a Brit was most proud of, what he loved to eat, and what he wanted to put at the centre of his business. It didn't take long before Pie Eyed was born, and the humble pie began flying the British flag amongst all the other cuisines on the street food scene.

It goes without saying that their home-made pastry is all-butter, their vegetables are locally sourced and their meat comes from a neighbouring butcher, of course. The most important thing for Pie Eyed is concentrating on one thing and executing it perfectly. No myriad fancy flavours and exotic ingredients, just four fantastic flavours that are real crowd-pleasers.

Beef brisket with Black Sheep Ale and chilli chorizo jam, Cheddar with caramelised red onion, chicken with white wine and tarragon, and chicken with bacon and pistachio. There you have the four classics, and it's clear why people have a hard time choosing which one to pick!

PIE EYED

BEEF BRISKET, BLACK SHEEP ALE AND CHILLI CHORIZO JAM

WITH LOCAL BEEF BRISKET AND BLACK SHEEP ALE, THESE ARE TRULY YORKSHIRE PIES. CHORIZO JAM MAKES A FANTASTIC ADDITION, AND IT IS READILY AVAILABLE FROM LOTS OF ARTISAN PRODUCERS. MAKES 4 INDIVIDUAL PIES OR 1 FAMILY PIE

FOR THE PASTRY:

250g plain flour

125g unsalted butter

5g parsley, finely chopped

A pinch of salt

50ml water

1 egg, beaten, to glaze

FOR THE FILLING:

50g plain flour

5g mustard powder

20g salt

30g pepper

400g beef brisket, diced

50ml oil

50g butter

2 brown onions, sliced

3 cloves garlic, chopped

2 carrots, diced

200ml Black Sheep Ale

200ml beef stock

75g tomato purée

20ml Henderson's Relish

20g parsley, finely chopped

100g mushrooms

2 sweet potatoes, diced

Chilli chorizo jam

To make the pastry, mix the flour, butter, parsley and a pinch of salt gently in a food mixer until it has a breadcrumb consistency. Add the water, little by little, until the dough begins to hold together. You may not need all of the water.

Place dough onto a lightly floured surface and very gently knead four or five times. Be careful not over-work the pastry, as this reduces the crumbliness of the pastry. Roll the pastry into a ball, wrap in cling film and refrigerate until needed, but for at least 30 minutes.

Preheat the oven to 180°C.

To make the filling, mix the flour and mustard powder and season with salt and pepper. Add the beef and evenly coat in the flour mixture.

Heat the oil and butter in a frying pan and add the beef. Cook the beef, in batches, over a high temperature until it has browned all over and transfer it to an ovenproof dish with a slotted spoon.

Add onions, garlic and carrots to the same frying pan and cook for 2-3 minutes. Add to the beef in the ovenproof dish. Add the Back Sheep Ale, stock, tomato purée and Henderson's Relish. Cook in the preheated oven for 3 hours, then add the chopped parsley, mushrooms and sweet potatoes. Reduce the temperature to 160°C and cook for a further 2 hours. Leave to cool completely.

When ready to assemble and cook the pies, preheat the oven to 200°C.

To assemble, roll out two-thirds of the pastry to about 3mm thick, and place into a greased family pie tin or four individual tins. Trim off the edges. Fill the pies two-thirds full with the cooled filling and add a dollop of chilli chorizo jam in the middle. Egg-wash the edges of the pastry.

Roll out the rest of the pastry, and cut into the shape of your pie tins to make pastry lids. Place the pastry lids on top of the pies, and crimp the edges together. Egg-wash the top, and leave to relax for about 10 minutes. Cook in the preheated oven for 25-30 minutes, until golden. Leave to cool for 15 minutes before taking the pies out of tins.

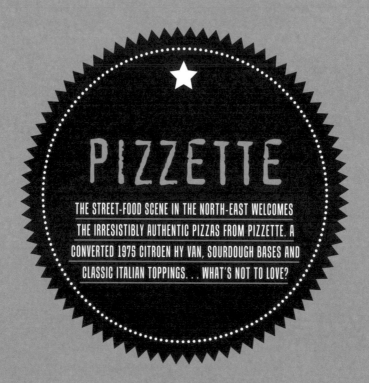

PIZZETTE

THE STREET-FOOD SCENE IN THE NORTH-EAST WELCOMES
THE IRRESISTIBLY AUTHENTIC PIZZAS FROM PIZZETTE. A
CONVERTED 1975 CITROEN HY VAN, SOURDOUGH BASES AND
CLASSIC ITALIAN TOPPINGS. . . WHAT'S NOT TO LOVE?

Small but oh so perfectly formed – a pizzette is a small pizza, the ideal size for one person to eat from a street food van. Made to order within 2 minutes, Mick and Matt of Pizzette have been wowing foodies and market-goers across the North-East with their classic Italian mini pizzas.

The sourdough is proved for an astonishing 20 hours to give it the distinct taste and texture that Pizzette's loyal customers adore. Made with classic Italian tipo "00" flour, the dough is hand-stretched before being topped and cooked to order. San Marzano tomatoes from Italy are used for the sauce, enhanced with just a little seasoning and extra virgin olive oil.

The toppings represent a true taste of Italy, with something to tempt every taste bud. For some classic Italian flavours, the Calabria is a popular choice, with fiery nduja, creamy mozzarella and aromatic basil, or try the Tuscan with fennel sausage, oregano and chilli. For those who don't like a tomato

base, Pizzette offer some traditional bianco pizzas, such as Maiale (pork belly, giroles and oregano) and the intriguing Pera (pear, pecorino, honeycomb and rocket).

The menu is tried and tested and has been carefully developed over many years, but of course you can always ask the chefs to put together something a bit different for you – such is the beauty of everything being freshly made to order!

With such a diverse range of pizzas on offer, it's no surprise that the converted 1975 Citroen HY van draws crowds and queues wherever it pulls up. Sourced from France, it was converted in the UK to house a wood-fired oven in the back, which heats up to 500 °C and allows Mick and Matt to cook pizzettes in just a couple of minutes. The resulting pizzas are so irresistible they tend to be consumed in a similar amount of time – perfect for feeding hungry guests at weddings and parties.

PIZZETTE

PIZZETTE

WORK

(0191) 232 5533
PIZZETTE.CO.UK

PIZZETTE ✶
6" WOODFIRED PIZZA

· WILD BOAR, RICOTTA ARTICHOKE & ROSEMARY
· MARGHERITA
· GARLIC, THYME, ONION
· PEPPERONI
· NDUJA & BASIL
· HAM, MUSHROOM & OREGANO
· GOAT'S CHEESE, PARMA HAM & ROCKET

PIZZETTE

PIZZA CINGHIALE

CINGHIALE TRANSLATES AS WILD BOAR AND WE GET OUR WILD BOAR SALAMI FROM A DELICATESSEN IN LONDON, CALLED VALLEBONA, WHO IMPORT QUALITY SARDINIAN PRODUCTS. WE USE SAN MARZANO TOMATOES THAT ARE GROWN AROUND MOUNT VESUVIUS. THESE ARE AVAILABLE TO BUY IN THE UK AND ARE WORTH SEEKING OUT FOR THE TASTIEST PIZZA SAUCE.

MAKES 12

FOR THE PIZZA DOUGH:

560g tipo flour "00"

1g fresh yeast

1 tsp sea salt

330ml water

FOR THE PIZZA SAUCE:

Extra virgin olive oil

Tinned San Marzano tomatoes, crushed

Salt and black pepper

FOR THE TOPPING:

Fior di latte mozzarella

Sheep's ricotta

Wild boar salami

Sprigs of fresh rosemary

Extra virgin olive oil

Mix together the flour, yeast and salt. Add the water and knead for about 20 minutes, until you have a shiny smooth dough. Cover and place in the fridge to slow-prove for a minimum of 20 hours; this is to give the sour taste.

Divide the dough into pieces the size of golf balls. Allow to prove for a second time in an ambient environment to slow rise.

To make the topping, stir a little olive oil into the tomatoes and season with salt and pepper.

Just before cooking, shape the base by taking one ball of dough and pushing out the base from the middle outwards, taking care to leave air in the edges. This will form the famous crust, which the Italians call the 'cornicione'.

Top the base with some of the sauce, add a small amount of fior di latte mozzarella, a couple of dollops of sheep's ricotta, 4-5 thin slices of the wild boar salami, a sprig of fresh rosemary and some extra virgin olive oil.

We slide this into our 100% log-burning oven at 450-500°C for 1 minute, then turn it around for 30-40 seconds. We then lift it up to the top of the oven just to give it a little char, then it's ready to eat. At home, cook it on a preheated pizza stone or baking tray at 220°C for about 10 minutes, until the dough is risen and cooked.

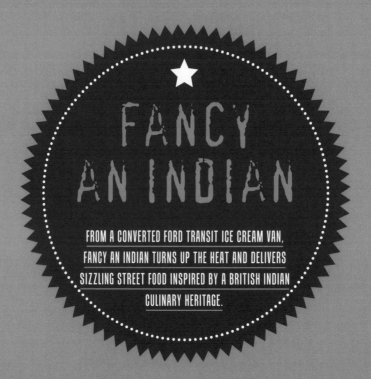

FANCY AN INDIAN

FROM A CONVERTED FORD TRANSIT ICE CREAM VAN, FANCY AN INDIAN TURNS UP THE HEAT AND DELIVERS SIZZLING STREET FOOD INSPIRED BY A BRITISH INDIAN CULINARY HERITAGE.

Like many passionate foodies, founder of Fancy an Indian, Bali Maman's early childhood meals stick firmly in her memories. A British Indian whose parents had moved here in the 1960s, Bali remembers tucking into her mum's home-made dhal or stuffed parathas as fondly as she remembers evening meals of frozen crispy pancakes and fish finger sandwiches.

Her love of cooking was inspired by her mum, who turned her hand to creating amazing Indian recipes using British staples. Spicy egg curry or spinach with pork luncheon meat are a couple of the favourites that shaped Bali's early food memories. Cue the pilchard curry, which was a classic in Bali's house, just as it was across many British Indian homes, and a recipe that she has adapted and developed as she has grown up. Sound unusual?

Granted it's not a traditional Indian curry, but in so many ways it sums up Bali's family's experiences of merging their Indian heritage with their home in the UK. Spices are crushed, ground and blended into a curry paste, fragranced with tamarind and cooled

with fresh yoghurt, leading to delightful aromas wafting from the kitchen. Then, to finish it off, canned pilchards – the little red tin symbolic of frugal post-war Britain.

Like her mum, Bali loves to cook and, like all good cooks, she loves to eat, too. Always trying new things, learning about new ingredients and exploring recipes, she knew that a career in food was her dream. So in May 2014, she took the plunge. Bali left her well-paid career in management in the NHS and bought an old Ford Transit ice cream van, which eventually became the 'wrapmobile'.

The Fancy an Indian 'wrapmobile' can be spotted at many festivals and events, and is a great addition to private parties. Indian street food classics that pack a punch with flavour are served to spice-lovers. You can also attend one of the Fancy an Indian pop-up supper clubs, to savour something more than finger food, or even book Bali for a cooking class to learn a few secrets about Indian cooking to impress your own dinner guests.

Hello Gorgeous...
Fancy an Indian?
Freshly made
ROTI WRAPS
filled with
PILCHARD CURRY
PICKLES, SAUCES
& RELISHES.

THE WRAPMOBILE

FANCY an INDIAN?

BALI 1

GLENRYCK
PILCHARDS
IN TOMATO SAUCE

FANCY an INDIAN?

FANCY
an
INDIAN?

INDIAN STREET FOOD

FANCY AN INDIAN

PILCHARD CURRY

THIS RECIPE USES MY FOOL-PROOF METHOD FOR CREATING A BASIC CURRY SAUCE, WHICH USES AN ONION BASE, 3 WET INGREDIENTS (GARLIC, GINGER AND CHILLIES), 3 DRY INGREDIENTS (GARAM MASALA, TURMERIC AND SALT) AND A "CURRY CARRIER", WHICH CAN BE VARIOUS LIQUIDS. THIS DISH IS ONE OF MY FAVOURITES TO REPRESENT MY BRITISH-ASIAN HERITAGE – AND ONE THAT MY FRIENDS ALWAYS ASK ME TO MAKE! SERVES 2.

FOR THE ONION BASE:

2 onions, chopped

1 tbsp ghee, butter or oil

FOR THE "3 WET INGREDIENTS"

3-4 cloves garlic, crushed

A thumb-sized piece of ginger

1-2 chillies, chopped, or more to taste

FOR THE "3 DRY INGREDIENTS"

1 tsp garam masala

1 tsp turmeric

Salt, to taste

FOR THE "CURRY CARRIER", PILCHARDS AND VEGETABLES

1 can of pilchards (in tomato sauce)

3 small potatoes, chopped into quarters

A cup of garden peas

TO SERVE

Rice or roti

Yoghurt

Pickles

Tamarind sauce

Fresh coriander

Fry the onions in the ghee, butter or oil until translucent and just starting to caramelize at the edges.

Make a wet paste out of the 3 wet ingredients (garlic, ginger and chillies) and add to the onions. Fry for 5 minutes.

Add the 3 dry ingredients (garam masala, turmeric and salt).

Remove the pilchards from the tin and set aside. Half-fill the empty pilchard tin with water to make 'pilchardy water' and add this to the spiced onions. Add the potatoes and cook until they are soft.

Add the pilchards and avoid stirring to keep the fish intact. Add the peas and cook to heat through.

Serve with rice or in a roti wrap with yoghurt, pickles, tamarind sauce and fresh coriander.

MY BASIC "3 WET/3 DRY" CURRY SAUCE RECIPE

You can use the basic recipe above of an onion base, 3 wet ingredients (garlic, ginger and chillies), 3 dry ingredients (garam masala, turmeric and salt) and a "curry carrier" to make all sorts of curries. Swap the curry carrier (here it is pilchard water) for coconut milk, cream, stock, tamarind, tomatoes (fresh or tinned), water or yoghurt, and simply add meat, fish and/or vegetables and simmer until cooked. Scale the recipe up or down as desired and adjust the chillies to taste.

PERCY & LILY'S

MEET PERCY, A 1969 GREY H VAN, AND LILY, A 1954 RARE SPLIT SCREEN YELLOW VAN – TOGETHER THESE TWO CITREON H VANS ARE THE HOME OF ONE OF SHEFFIELD'S MOST ENTICING STREET FOOD BUSINESSES.

The brains behind Percy & Lily's belong to Trudi Colman and Justine Twigge. Percy is named after Trudi's grandfather, who worked as a chef and housekeeper for the same wealthy estate owners for a staggering 65 years. His cakes were legendary and he handed his love for cooking and baking to his granddaughter. Lily bears the name of Justine's grandmother, a tremendous cook and baker who worked in prestigious hotel kitchens and as a silver service waitress. Today, these inspirational family members live on in the two characterful Citreons.

Trudi and Justine met in 2001 at Sheffield Hallam University. They had both worked in food and catering in the past, giving them a solid basis for a friendship that would inspire world travels and an enormously successful business partnership.

In 2006, they set off on a life-changing trip. Following the death of a close friend, they left their jobs and, armed with an A4 ledger book, began an epic journey around the world collecting ideas and inspiration. It soon became apparent that their collective ideas all centred on food. After several bottles of red wine on a rainy day in Queensland, they came up with a selection of world menus that would, on their return to the UK, become the basis for Homemade, their first business together.

Another travelling expedition followed the sale of this successful venture, and more ideas developed in South America. The vans were the result of this brainstorming trip and the business concept began coming together. In January 2014, Percy & Lily's became a reality, and the two vans are taking Sheffield's street food scene by storm. Refusing to be pigeon-holed to one type of cuisine, the menus reflect Trudi and Justine's exotic travels and love of food and drink from all over the world.

Their unprecedented success shows just how adventurous Sheffield is becoming when it comes to food. With a jam-packed calendar of street food markets, weddings and private parties, as well as eclectic events such as drive-in cinema nights and their Street Food Northern Soul night, Percy and Lily are busy little vans! And with, at the last count, 1034 quesadillas made so far, and bookings increasing each week, Trudi and Justine have had their work cut out too.

However, for this ambitious pair, there is always a new adventure around the corner. Next up, their recent purchase, The Hide – a warehouse-style urban space – will become home to Street Food Friday... get ready Sheffield...

the
HIDE
by Percy & Lily

Prosecco
Bar

PERCY AND LILY'S
ARGENTINIAN CHORIPÁN

CHORIPÁN IS A TYPE OF SANDWICH WITH SAUSAGE POPULAR IN ARGENTINA AND OTHER SOUTH AMERICAN COUNTRIES. THE NAME COMES FROM THE COMBINATION OF THE NAMES OF ITS INGREDIENTS: A GRILLED CHORIZO STYLE SAUSAGE AND A PAN (BREAD). THE CLASSIC ARGENTINE CHORIPÁN CONSISTS OF A SAUSAGE MADE OUT OF BEEF AND PORK, HOT OFF THE GRILL, SPLIT DOWN THE MIDDLE, AND SERVED ON A ROLL. IT IS CUSTOMARY TO ADD SAUCES ON THE BREAD, MOST LIKELY THE 'HOUSE' CHIMICHURRI WHICH IS A SALSA-STYLE DRESSING MADE WITH PARSLEY, LEMON, GARLIC AND VINEGAR AND IS UNIQUE TO EACH FAMILY OR RESTAURANT. WE HAVE A SAUSAGE MADE TO OUR RECIPE BY OUR LOCAL BUTCHER. HOWEVER, WE ALSO OFFER 3-HOUR COOKED BEEF BRISKET IN OUR 'CHORIPÁN' AND SERVE IT WITH OUR UNIQUE HOUSE CHIMICHURRI AND THEY GO DOWN A STORM! TRADITIONALLY CHIMICHURRI IS GREEN, BUT WE'VE ADDED A SWEET RED PEPPER TO OURS.

SERVES 8

FOR THE BEEF BRISKET:

1.8kg beef brisket, preferably from a butcher

400ml red wine

400ml water

2 tbsp tomato ketchup

2 tbsp dark brown sugar

2 cloves garlic, finely chopped

½ tsp chilli flakes or ½ fresh red chilli, finely chopped

3 tbsp smoked paprika

1 tbsp dried Italian mixed herbs

1 level tsp cayenne pepper

1 level tsp salt

2 tbsp Tabasco sauce

8 tbsp Worcestershire sauce

FOR THE CHIMICHURRI:

A bunch of flat leaf parsley

8 cloves garlic

Juice of 1 lemon

300ml olive oil

100ml white wine vinegar

2 shallots, finely diced

1 red pepper, finely diced

½ teaspoon salt, or to taste

½ teaspoon black pepper, or to taste

TO SERVE:

8 brioche rolls or burger buns

Preheat the oven to 160°C. Sear the beef brisket in a hot pan, fat-side down, until brown and slightly charred. Put the wine, water, ketchup and sugar into a large roasting tray and mix all the other beef brisket ingredients in a bowl to form a paste. Rub the paste all over the beef. Place the beef, fat-side up, into the wine and water mixture. Cover with a lid and foil to seal in the steam. If you have no lid, just cover tightly with a double layer of foil ensuring no air can escape. Roast in the preheated oven for 1 hour 30 minutes.

After this time, check that the liquid has not evaporated (add a little more water if needed), cover tightly, reduce the oven temperature to 150°C and continue to roast for a further 1 hour 30 minutes.

After the total 3 hours, turn the oven off and either let the beef sit for a further 40 minutes steaming in its juices, or remove it and place it on to a warm plate, covered, for 30 minutes before slicing.

For the chimichurri, blitz the parsley, garlic, lemon juice, oil and vinegar together in a food processor or blender to make a paste. Mix in the finely diced shallots and red pepper by hand. Season to taste.

Griddle or toast 8 brioche buns or white burger rolls, before filling each with your sliced beef brisket, topped with the chimichurri. It's a firm favourite with our punters. We also offer a vegetarian version with roasted squash in garlic and oregano, topped with melted mozzarella and the chimichurri.

PERCY AND LILY'S
LEBANESE FLATBREAD

FOR THE ROASTED AUBERGINE LABNA:

1 small aubergine

1 whole garlic bulb

½ bunch of fresh mint

Juice of ½ lemon

300ml full-fat Greek yoghurt

2 tbsp tahini

2 tsp sumac

FOR THE ZA'ATAR:

4 tbsp sesame seeds

4 tbsp chopped fresh oregano

4 tsp dried marjoram

4 tsp ground sumac

1 tsp sea salt

4 tsp ground cumin

FOR THE LAMB :

3 white onions, finely diced

750g minced lamb

½ tsp chilli flakes or ½ fresh red chilli, finely chopped

3 tbsp Lebanese Spice Blend (lemon oil, sumac, pomegranate seeds, parsley, roasted cumin and coriander seeds)

1 level tsp salt, + extra if needed

2 tins chopped tomatoes

1 tbsp sumac

1 tbsp ground cinnamon

2 tbsp tomato purée

100g raisins

Olive oil, for frying

TO SERVE:

8 flatbreads

Good-quality garlic olive oil, ready-made harissa sauce or tomato sauce

A jar of cumin-infused black olives

8 handfuls of spinach

1 lemon, cut into 8 segments

8 tsp sumac

OUR LOVE OF MIDDLE EASTERN FOOD GOES BACK A LONG WAY. WE CREATED THIS FLATBREAD AND THE FIRST TIME WE OFFERED IT, WE SOLD OUT IN RECORD TIME. IN FACT THIS IS PROBABLY OUR MOST POPULAR MENU. WE HAVE THE FLATBREADS MADE LOCALLY ON THE MORNING WE TRADE, AND THEY ARE FANTASTIC. THE TOPPINGS WOULD WORK ON A VARIETY OF FLATBREADS, PITAS OR EVEN PIZZA DOUGH. SO LET'S CUT TO THE CHASE. . .

SERVES 8

For the roasted aubergine labna, preheat the oven to 180°C. Roast the aubergine whole alongside the whole garlic bulb for 30 minutes. Allow to cool before cutting in half and scooping the flesh into a food processor or blender. Peel 6 cloves of the roasted garlic and add to the blender with the mint and lemon juice. Blitz for 30 seconds. Add the Greek yoghurt, sumac and tahini, and blitz for a further 30 seconds. Season with a little salt and pepper if required and refrigerate for 30 minutes or until needed.

For the za'atar, toast the sesame seeds in a dry frying pan over a high heat for 1-2 minutes. Place all the ingredients in a blender and process until finely mixed. Store in a jar for up to a week. (You can use the za'atar on home-made hummus, 3-egg omelettes and on a lovely fresh vine tomato salad with mint, black olives and griddled halloumi cheese. It's like the Middle Eastern 'salt and pepper' and they use it on many dishes.)

For the Lebanese Lamb, fry the diced onions in a little oil until translucent, then add the minced lamb, breaking it down with a wooden spoon as it cooks. Cook for 30-45 minutes until all the natural fat and juices are gone. You can use a cup and drain off the excess fat after 25 minutes to speed up this process.

When the lamb is a dry mixture, add the chilli flakes or fresh chilli, spice blend, salt and chopped tomatoes. Stir in well and bring to a simmer. Cook for a further 15 minutes before adding the sumac, cinnamon and tomato purée. Cook for 10 minutes more until you have a rich mixture with a thick sauce. Add the raisins and season to taste. Leave to one side for 10 minutes before serving.

To serve, warm each flatbread in a dry frying pan, under the grill or on a griddle or barbeque for 30-45 seconds. Place it on a board or flat plate and build up the flatbread. We make a tomato, parsley and harissa base (a bit like a pizza base) but you can use garlic olive oil or a ready-made harrisa sauce or tomato sauce. Thinly spread the sauce on the flatbread using a pastry brush. Spoon 2-3 tablespoons of minced lamb onto the bread and spread it roughly. Add three dollops of aubergine labna, and in-between the labna add 8-10 infused black olives and a handful of baby spinach leaves. Squeeze a segment of fresh lemon across the top of each, and add a teaspoon of the za'atar and a teaspoon of sumac. Serve immediately like a pizza or roll it and eat it like a burrito. It really is a taste sensation. We love them and so do our foodie followers!

KITSCH'N CRÊPE CO.

SAM AND PAUL ARE HITTING THE STREETS OF THE NORTH-EAST WITH THEIR UNIQUE CRÊPES. WHETHER IT'S SWEET OR SAVOURY, THERE IS SOMETHING SPECIAL ON THE MENU AT KITSCH'N CRÊPE CO.

There's nothing quite like a fresh crêpe for a true taste of street food magic. Watching skilled crêpe makers swirl the batter into thin French pancakes before their eyes is what makes customers' mouths water and brings smiles to their faces. It was this irresistible theatre of making fresh crêpes to order that inspired Sam and Paul to launch their Kitsch'n Crêpe Co. street food business.

Racking up many years of experience between them, it was a natural move for this talented pair. Sam is currently Kitchen Manager at The Tyne Bar and previously part-owned Kitsch'n Café in the Jesmond area, where crêpes were a speciality. Paul owns a popular B&B, Summerville Guest House, where he is famous for cooking his delicious breakfasts.

The menu is far from your traditional list of tried and tested options. Inspiration is taken from around the word, with savoury specials such as Piri Piri (spicy chicken with spinach, peppers, cheese and jalapeños), Santana (sweet potato and pepper chilli with cheese and sour cream) and Champignon (creamy garlic mushrooms with mozzarella).

For those with a sweet tooth, it's difficult to choose between such delights as the Funky Monkey (Nutella and mini marshmallows), Lemony Snicket (lemon and lavender sugar) and The Queen's Peach (caramelized peaches with toffee sauce and cream). Although you can always go for something more traditional, if you prefer – what's not to love about a classic lemon, sugar and butter crêpe or one coated in home-made salted caramel?

Although Kitsch'n Crêpe Co. are busy popping up at food fairs, festivals and various events across the North-east, they are also available for booking for private parties and weddings, where they can offer a menu to suit you. Their gazebo and impressive crêpe plates will cause a stir at any event, and certainly put smiles on guests' faces as they tuck into the freshly made treats.

SAVOURY CREPES

- **MEXICAN**
  CHILLI CON CARNE
  CHEESE + JALAPENOS

- **CREPE MONSIEUR**
  HAM + CHEDDAR

- **SPINACH + RICOTTA**
  WITH TOASTED PINE
  NUTS

- **ITALIAN JOB**
  MOZZARELLA PESTO
  SUNDRIED TOMATO +
  SPINACH

SWEET CREPES

- **MAPLE + PECAN**

- **NUTELLA + MINI
  MARSHMALLOWS**

- **STRAWBERRY SUNDAE**
  STRAWBERRIES NUTS
  CHOCOLATE GANACHE +
  CREAM

- **BANOFFEE**
  TOFFEE BANANA CREAM
  + GINGER BISCUITS

- **LEMON + SUGAR**

- **COCOCABANA**
  NUTELLA TOAS
  CINNAMO

SPINACH

SWEET CREPES

- **MAPLE + PECAN**

- **NUTELLA + MINI
  MARSHMALLOWS**

Kitsch'n crepe co

KITSCH'N CRÊPE CO.

STRAWBERRY SUNDAE CRÊPES WITH CHOCOLATE GANACHE FILLING

WE USE ACORN DAIRY ORGANIC MILK, EGGS AND FLOUR TO MAKE OUR CRÊPE BATTER. WE MAKE OUR CRÊPES TO ORDER AND ASSEMBLE THEM DIRECTLY ON THE CRÊPE PLATE TO ENSURE THE FRESHEST AND MOST DELICIOUS CRÊPES. UNFILLED CRÊPES CAN BE WRAPPED IN CLING FILM OR PARCHMENT AND KEPT IN THE FRIDGE FOR 3 DAYS.

MAKES 12

FOR THE CRÊPE BATTER:

60g unsalted butter, plus extra for frying

2 large eggs

650ml milk

300g plain four

FOR THE CHOCOLATE GANACHE FILLING:

225g dark chocolate, above 40% cocoa solids

125ml double cream

TO FINISH:

Strawberries, sliced

Squirty cream

Chopped nuts

Chocolate drizzle

White crêpe cones, from R&R packaging (optional)

For the crêpe batter, melt the butter and allow to cool slightly. Add the eggs to the milk in a large bowl and sieve in the flour. Using a hand blender, blitz to a smooth liquid, getting rid of any lumps.

Add in the melted butter. I find it better to refrigerate the mixture at this stage.

Heat a seasoned 8-inch crêpe pan (or frying pan) and add some butter (we use Frylite to spray our crêpe plates, so either is fine). Swirl the pan with the butter or oil and wipe out any excess.

Using a ladle or jug, pour a thin layer of crêpe batter into the pan. Quickly swirl the pan before the mixture sets; it should only take a minute. To flip over to the other side, run a palette knife gently around the edges to loosen, then flip the crêpe. Don't worry if the first one doesn't work, they always get better! Set aside while you finish the batch.

For the chocolate ganache, heat the cream gently in a pan. Add the chocolate and heat until melted, dark and smooth. The ganache can now be added straight to the crêpes or allowed to cool.

At Kitsch'n Crêpe Co., after we have flipped the crêpe and cooked the second side, we spread it with ganache and cover in slices of strawberry. We fold it in half and roll into a cone shape. Then we pop it straight into a crêpe cone, squirt the cream onto the top, sprinkle with nuts and drizzle with chocolate if required.

If making at home, you could do it like this in the pan or even reheat the prepared crêpe in the microwave. Spread it with ganache, cover with sliced strawberries then fold into a triangle and serve on a plate with a squirt of cream on the top, it's up to you!

GINGER BAKERS

FROM KENDAL FARMERS MARKET TO SUPPLYING EVENTS
ALL OVER THE COUNTRY, GINGER BAKERS ARE TAKING
A TASTE OF THE LAKE DISTRICT TO STREET
FOOD MARKETS ACROSS THE UK.

From a start-up business in a home kitchen to a busy bakery supplying markets, shops and events all over the UK, Ginger Bakers has acquired an abundance of awards since it began life in 2006. With a background in design, a qualification as an art therapist and a keen interest in keeping up with food trends, when Lisa Smith started her own baking business, she put her enthusiasm for all things creative into baking cakes and wrapping them lovingly from her Lake District home.

Coming from a family of entrepreneurs and inspired by cakes made by her grandmother and mother, Lisa set about developing a range of unique cakes and bakes. Her creative background is evident in the eye-catching packaging and the quirky names reveal the importance of family to Lisa's business – the 'ginger bakers' being a reference to her two red-haired children, who each have a product named after them in 'Ginger Jake' and 'Chocolate Nancy'.

Despite the unprecedented growth over the past nine years, Lisa has kept quality and integrity at the core of Ginger Bakers. The beauty of the Lake District,

the incredible bounty of produce it offers and the close-knit community of local businesses inspired Lisa and her loyal team of employees to keep their products as 'local' as possible – Lyth Valley damsons are used in the deliciously different Chocolate Damson Brownies and sourcing free-range eggs from nearby farms ensures that they are as fresh as can be. Always keen to satisfy all customers' needs, they offer a wide range of gluten-free cakes and will aim to fulfil any special dietary requirement.

The Ginger Bakers bakery is a busy and vibrant environment. Although Lisa and her team now prepare a huge amount of cake to order, everything is still made completely by hand – and it always will be. As well as the day-to-day baking each week the talented team spend a lot of time and effort discussing new ideas and working on product development. They keep an eye on the emerging trends and are constantly coming up with fantastic new recipes. Watch out for their regularly changing list of products, which appear at Kendal Farmers Market, as well as at markets across the country from the Lake District to London.

GINGER BAKERS

CHOCOLATE NANCY

UNIQUE TO GINGER BAKERS, THIS IS AN EYE-CATCHING CHEEKY OAT BAR CRAMMED WITH FRUIT-AND-NUT GOODNESS AND TOPPED WITH A SMOTHERING OF PLAIN CHOCOLATE. YOU CAN BE CREATIVE AND EXCHANGE ANY OF THE FRUITS AND NUTS FOR THOSE OF YOUR CHOICE AND CREATE A UNIQUE BAR OF YOUR OWN. SERVES 12.

150g salted butter

220g sweetened condensed milk

1 tbsp finely grated lemon zest

170g jumbo oats (gluten-free, if you prefer)

140g dried cranberries

120g dried apricots, chopped finely

120g sultanas

60g desiccated coconut

60g whole blanched almonds, chopped

60g shelled pistachios, chopped

FOR THE TOPPING:

100g good-quality plain chocolate

60g salted butter

A handful of dried cranberries and pistachios, chopped finely

Line a tray bake tin (approximately 23cm x 23cm) with baking parchment so that it covers the base and the sides.

Melt the butter and the condensed milk in a pan over a gentle heat until the two are well combined. Stir the mixture continuously, making sure that it doesn't burn. Set aside to cool slightly.

Measure out all the dry ingredients into a large bowl and give them a good stir, folding them over so that they are all evenly combined. Pour over the melted butter and condensed milk mixture and mix well. The mixture should be slightly sticky.

Pour the mixture into the lined tin and spread it evenly, pushing it into the corners and making sure it is pressed well and is flat and smooth on top. Chill in the fridge for about 30 minutes. You may want to add some more pressure to help the pressing by placing another piece of silicone paper on top of the tray of mixture and putting a weight on top. (This could be something like a small stack of books, or another tray with a bag of sugar in it.)

In the meantime you can be preparing the topping. The chocolate topping can be made either in a bain marie or in the microwave. Either way, make sure you don't overheat the chocolate, as this results in it appearing dull and without its attractive shine. Place the butter and chocolate in a microwavable bowl and heat for 30 seconds at a time, stirring well between each heating, until both are melted and well combined.

Take the chilled base mixture out of the refrigerator and pour the chocolate mixture over the top, tilting the tray from side to side until it is completely covered. Sprinkle with the cranberries and pistachios before the chocolate sets. Allow the topping to completely set then cut into your preferred size pieces and serve. Chocolate Nancy will keep well for up to 2 weeks if put in an airtight container in a cool place.

KHOO'S HOT SAUCE

FROM SELLING THE FIRST BATCH OF HOT SAUCE FROM HIS CAR BOOT TO BEING STOCKED IN RETAILERS ACROSS YORKSHIRE, KHOO'S HOT SAUCE IS SPICING UP HOME-COOKING ALL OVER THE NORTH OF ENGLAND.

A love of chillies isn't something new for Alex Khoo, who has been growing them at home for over ten years. A keen cook, Alex has not only experimented with growing various varieties of the spicy little peppers, but he's also spent years creating fiery recipes with them in the kitchen. It wasn't until August 2012 that he took the plunge to turn his hobby (which was now becoming quite expensive to maintain!) into a business.

Finding a house with a garden big enough for Alex's chilli plants turned out to be no mean feat, but after two years of searching, he finally had his polytunnel in place in his sunny Sheffield garden and Khoo's Hot House was officially up and running.

As far as growing chillies is concerned, the British climate is challenging to say the least. Luckily, Alex's dedication to his fiery crops is top-notch. It sees him grow them indoors from January to May, before moving them outside to the polytunnel.

During a good season, he can harvest his 30 species (he favours the hottest varieties to get the best flavour in his products) of chilli peppers right up until December, before starting all over again in January with the next crop.

Everything is done by hand, from growing and harvesting to cooking and bottling the sauces. Alex smokes some of his Mexican varieties for his Heavy Smoker chipotle sauce. There are currently six sauces on sale – not only in his native Sheffield, but throughout Yorkshire, Derbyshire and Manchester, too. There are also plans for some new sauces in the pipeline, so keep your eye out at the street food markets and local retailers around you for new varieties of Khoo's Hot Sauce in the near future.

KHOO'S HOT SAUCE

KHOO'S JERK CHICKEN

JERK CHICKEN IS A POPULAR DISH AT STREET FOOD MARKETS, BUT IT'S EASY TO MAKE AT HOME WITH THE HELP OF SOME KHOO'S NORTHERN BEACON HOT SAUCE. YOU CAN COOK THE CHICKEN IN A SMOKER OR IN THE OVEN – BOTH METHODS ARE GIVEN HERE. SERVES 4.

4 chicken legs

1 large tomato, roughly chopped

1 tbsp honey

Basmati rice, to serve

10g preserved black beans

Mixed leaf salad, to serve

FOR THE MARINADE:

1 tbsp whole allspice

1 tsp ground nutmeg

1 tsp ground cinnamon

1 tsp paprika

1 tsp sea salt

½ tsp ground black pepper

2 tbsp freshly chopped thyme

3 spring onions

4 cloves garlic

40ml light soy sauce

30ml lime juice

60ml Khoo's Northern Beacon hot sauce

For the marinade, use a spice grinder or food processor to blend all the dried spices to a powder.

Add the thyme, spring onions, garlic, soy sauce, lime juice and Khoo's Northern Beacon hot sauce and blend to a paste. At this point, reserve one-third of the jerk paste and set aside.

Rub the remaining two-thirds of the paste into the chicken legs, ensuring you get the paste worked into the meat and under the skin where possible. Let the chicken marinate for a minimum of 2 hours, or overnight if you have time.

You can cook the chicken in the oven or in a smoker.

OVEN METHOD

Preheat the oven to 200°C. Place the chicken on a wire rack grill pan and bake in the preheated oven for 30 minutes to brown the chicken. Keep an eye on the legs and turn the heat down to 175°C if the jerk paste shows signs of charring. Once the chicken is browned, turn the heat down to 175°C and cook for a further 15-30 minutes, until the juices run clear or the internal temperature reaches 74°C.

SMOKER METHOD

If you have the facilities to hot smoke and fancy that authentic flavour, heat your smoker to 220°C and cook the chicken legs for 3-4 hours or until they reach an internal temperature of 74°C. Cherry wood works beautifully with this recipe.

While the chicken is cooking, add the tomato and honey to the reserved jerk paste and blend to a smooth sauce. Simmer the sauce in a small pan for 10 minutes, adding a little water if necessary to thin the sauce to a pourable consistency.

Add the preserved black beans to the basmati rice before cooking it according to the packet instructions. Plate up your jerk chicken with black bean rice and mixed leaf salad. Pour the sweetened jerk sauce over the chicken and rice and it's ready to serve.

LIBERTY FOODS

CURRIED SCOTCH EGGS

MEET DAMIAN BOWER AND SIMON BARNES, THE HARD-WORKING TEAM BEHIND THE SUCCESSFUL LIBERTY FOODS. DAMIAN'S IMPRESSIVE EXPERIENCE IN BUTCHERY, FRONT OF HOUSE AND AS A CHEF HAD GIVEN HIM THE WELL-ROUNDED SKILLS HE NEEDED TO MAKE THE BOLD DECISION TO TAKE OVER THE LIBERTY FOODS FARM SHOP ON BASLOW ROAD IN TOTLEY. ALL HE NEEDED WAS A CHEF AND, WITH HIS BACKGROUND AS A BAKER, PASTRY CHEF AND HEAD CHEF, AND EXPERIENCE IN FRONT OF HOUSE AND KITCHEN MANAGEMENT, SIMON WAS THE PERFECT CANDIDATE. TOGETHER, THEY CREATED A BUSINESS THAT HAS BECOME A SHEFFIELD GEM. THINK PIES, PASTRIES, READY-MEALS, BLACK PUDDING – ALL HOME-MADE OF COURSE – AS WELL AS FREE-RANGE HEREFORD BEEF FROM BROADSTORTH FARM IN DORE AND DRY-CURED SMOKED BACON AND SALMON FROM THEIR OWN SMOKEHOUSE. THEY SUPPLY SHOPS, PUBS AND DELIS WITH THEIR HAND-MADE PRODUCE, FROM PORK PIES TO BAKEWELL PUDDINGS, NOT FORGETTING DAMIAN'S AWARD-WINNING SCOTCH EGGS. YOU'LL FIND THEM AT SHEFFIELD AND DERBYSHIRE FARMERS' MARKETS, OR JUST POP IN TO THE SHOP AT 253 BASLOW ROAD.

Spice up a classic Scotch egg with some curry powder. The key to the best flavour is buying good-quality eggs, sausage meat and curry powder. Serves 4

SCOTCH EGGS:

12 thick butcher's sausages, about 675g in weight

4 tbsp home-made curry powder or a good-quality shop-bought blend

150ml cold water

4 hen or duck eggs, soft-boiled

100g plain flour, seasoned with salt and pepper

2 eggs, beaten

150-200g panko breadcrumbs (or white bread, grated whilst frozen)

Skin the sausage and combine the meat, curry powder and water in a bowl. Mix thoroughly and divide into four meatballs.

Hold a meatball in the palm of one hand and hollow out the meatball with your other thumb. Place the egg inside and squeeze together to seal the meat around the egg, forming it into an egg-shape. Repeat with the other three eggs.

Dip the Scotch eggs into the flour, then the beaten egg and finally the breadcrumbs.

Heat the oil for deep-frying in a deep-fryer or heavy-bottomed pan to 170°C. Deep-fry the eggs for 7 minutes, then carefully remove and drain.

MAGPIE CAFE STREET FOOD

KNOWN THROUGHOUT YORKSHIRE AS ONE OF THE VERY BEST PLACES TO TUCK INTO FISH AND CHIPS, THE FAMOUS MAGPIE CAFÉ IN WHITBY IS NOW TAKING THEIR FINEST FISH AND SEAFOOD ONTO THE STREET.

When it comes to Britain's best fish and chips, the Magpie Café will always get a mention. The North Yorkshire seafood restaurant is easily spotted by its queue at the door, which is there all year round come rain or shine. With such demand for its famous seafood, the team at Magpie Café decided to offer a taste of their legendary fish in a new street food setting.

Located just 100 yards away, the Magpie Café Street Food stall offers an enticing menu of 'grab and go' classics, which are all perfect for holding in your hands and eating on the move as you stroll along the historic seafront. Of course you can find a bench and sit down with the food too – there is no rush when it comes to enjoying the freshest fish and shellfish in such a beautiful location.

Cod and brill are the local favourites for fish and chips, and it goes without saying that whatever fish you choose has been sustainably sourced from well-managed fishing grounds. The fish baps and fish wraps are perfect for the street food scene, simply wrapped in a napkin and devoured in the open air. There is something about the Whitby sea breeze that makes eating these hand-held treats really something special – or perhaps it's the special home-made sauces, such as the spicy seafood sauce, that are the key.

All the fish is cooked fresh on the stall – crisp, fresh and hot from the fryer. Not a soggy chip in sight! Piping hot scampi is popular too, along with those English seaside classics, cockles and mussels. Using the same fish and shellfish as the renowned restaurant, customers can rely on always getting the finest quality food, without the famous Magpie Café queue – perfect when your visit to Whitby is a short one. You can always visit their nearby fishmonger to take some fresh fish home with you afterwards – then have a go at making your own deliciously local fish bap.

MAGPIE'S
street food

MAGPIE'S
street food

XL Whitby Scampi Small

XL Whitby Scampi Large

Lemon Sole Goujons

Fish Fingers

Haddock Fish Cakes

White Bait

Pot of Crab Meat

Pot of Prawns

Whole Dressed Crab

Dressed Lobster

Specials

MAGPIE CAFÉ STREET FOOD
CRISPY COD BAP WITH SPICY SEAFOOD SAUCE

A POPULAR RECIPE FROM THE STREET FOOD STALL –
PERFECT FOR HOLDING IN YOUR HAND AS YOU STROLL AROUND
BEAUTIFUL WHITBY. SERVES 4.

250g plain flour

50g fine maize flour

1 tsp cornflour

1 heaped tsp cayenne pepper

Chilled water

800g cod fillet, cut into 16 strips

4 white baps or stotties

2 Little Gem lettuces

2 beef tomatoes, thinly sliced

2 dill gherkins, thinly sliced

Salt and white pepper

Oil, for deep frying

FOR THE SEAFOOD SAUCE:

2 tsp English mustard powder

1 tsp chilli powder

1 tsp mixed herbs

½ tsp ground nutmeg

½ tsp ground cumin

½ tsp ground coriander

½ tsp ground turmeric

50ml warm water

200ml mayonnaise

Make up the seafood sauce by blitzing the herbs and spices together with the warm water in a food processor and then add the mayonnaise and blitz until well mixed together. This is best done a couple of days beforehand – just pop it in the fridge and let the flavours develop and intensify.

To make the coating, combine 150g of the plain flour with the maize flour, cornflour and cayenne pepper. Mix the remainder of the flour with enough chilled water to form a batter that has the consistency of single cream.

Heat some oil in a deep pan (do not fill more than two-thirds full) to 180˚C. Season the pieces of cod with salt and pepper, then dip them through the batter and into the coating. Repeat this process so that the fish has been double coated, then carefully lay the cod into the oil and fry for around 3 minutes or until golden in colour (you may have to do this in smaller batches depending on the size of your pan). Once the fish has cooked, remove it carefully from the pan and place onto kitchen paper to drain.

To serve, slice open the baps and on the bottom half spread on the spicy seafood sauce generously, lay on the cod (four pieces per portion) then some Little Gem, sliced tomato and gherkin. Spread more sauce on the underneath of the top half of the bun, wrap in a napkin and away you go, taking in deep breaths of the Yorkshire coast sea air. Enjoy.

PIZZA LOCO

PERFECTLY CRISP, TRADITIONAL NEAPOLITAN PIZZAS WITH A HINT OF YORKSHIRE IN THE TOPPINGS – SOLD FROM THE BACK OF A STEAM ENGINE! NO WONDER PIZZA LOCO DRAWS IN THE CROWDS WHEREVER IT GOES...

Italian on the bottom and Yorkshire on the top – that's how Oliver Reynolds describes his Pizza Loco pizzas. The dough is made using Caputo flour imported from Italy and is left to rise slowly over 24 hours to create the crisp yet chewy texture with puffed-up crusts. The dough is topped with San Marzano tomatoes – nothing else comes close to the sweet, fleshy, Italian tomatoes for a true Neapolitan taste. In fact they are so good they need nothing more than a sprinkle of sea salt and a drizzle of extra virgin olive oil to create the tomato sauce.

So that's the Italian bit. As much as we all love simple mozzarella, Pizza Loco are taking on the Italians with their incredible Yorkshire toppings. Award-winning local cheeses create interesting flavour combinations that complement the sweet Italian bases. From Ribblesdale to Wensleydale, you'll find all sorts of Yorkshire cheeses cropping up on their unique menu. You won't find their chorizo in Napoli either; they put it together themselves and it's handmade in Yorkshire.

The thin-crust pizzas get their famous crisp yet chewy bases thanks to the iconic Pizza Loco oven. Oliver's business partner Paul Bulmer custom-built the crowd-pleasing street food trailer. He adapted a twin-axle cattle trailer, stripping it down and fitting it with a wood-burning oven. Based on centuries-old Italian design, the dome-shaped oven reaches searing temperatures of around 500°C, so it takes just 60 seconds to cook a pizza to perfection!

It was only once the oven was installed and they started firing it up with wood that they recognised the similarity to shovelling coal into the furnace at the back of a steam train. With this nostalgic idea in his mind, Paul set about remodelling the trailer into a jaw-dropping steam engine – and what a fabulous job he did! This glorious engine will be chugging along to many food markets around the North, when it's not busy wowing guests at weddings, parties and private events of course. With a busy calendar ahead, you ought to book them now for a slice of the action!

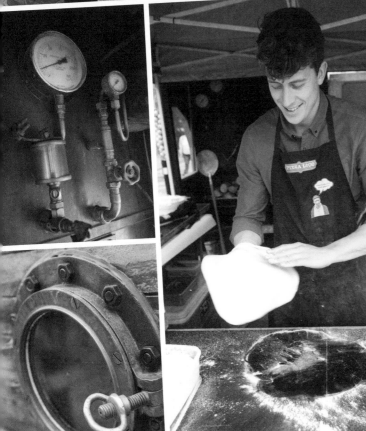

PIZZA LOCO

SHREDDED DUCK WITH HERB-INFUSED HONEY, BALSAMIC FIGS & BRIE

THIS PIZZA WORKS PERFECTLY WELL WITHOUT THE DUCK TOO, SO GOOD NEWS FOR VEGETARIANS. THE DOUGH TAKES AROUND 18-20 HOURS AT ROOM TEMP TO RISE SLOWLY, SO MAKE THIS AT ABOUT 8PM THE NIGHT BEFORE TO BE READY IN TIME FOR DINNER THE FOLLOWING EVENING. MAKES 1.

1 dough ball, left to prove for 1-2 hours

Flour, for dusting

1 dessertspoon extra virgin olive oil

60g fior di latte mozzarella, torn

5-6 slices Brie

2 pinches of fresh thyme leaves

1 dessertspoon runny honey

1 large, squidgy, very ripe fig

1 dessertspoon Balsamic vinegar

FOR THE DOUGH (MAKES 4 X 10 INCH BASES):

1g fresh yeast (0.6 active dry yeast)

300ml tepid water

1 dessertspoon extra virgin olive oil (optional)

500g '00' flour

15g sea salt

FOR THE DUCK:

1 duck leg (or breast if you can't get legs)

½ teaspoon juniper berries

½ teaspoon black peppercorns

1 bay leaf

1 tbsp sea salt

2 garlic cloves, crushed or finely chopped

For the dough, stir the yeast into the water until dissolved and add the olive oil. In a large (2 litre) mixing bowl, sift in the flour and add the salt. Combine the salt and flour with your fingertips before making a well in the centre. Fill the well with some of the liquid and, using a wooden spoon, begin stirring the walls of flour into the mixture so it thickens. As it thickens, gradually add the rest of the yeast mixture, and combine with the spoon for a minute or so. Now scrape the dough from the spoon back into the bowl, and swap the spoon for working the dough using only your fingers (dough builds up on the palms very easily). Work for a good 10 minutes to mop up all the flour, so the dough is roughly combined. It might look a little lumpy at this point, but don't worry. Lightly oil a clean bowl then place the dough in it before covering with cling film, and rest for 1 hour.

Flour a wooden board or surface and lay out the dough. Gently make a rough rectangle shape. Fold the four corners into the centre, one after the other. Repeat once more. The dough should now be much smoother. Oil a bowl that is twice the volume of the dough, and place the ball of dough in smooth-side up before rubbing a little oil over the top. Cover with cling film, and leave at room temp for 16-18 hours (at least 10 hours). Allow 1-2 hours longer if it's colder than room temperature.

Cut dough into four equal pieces using a sharp knife, and repeat the folding method as before. Then shape into balls. At this point, the dough balls can be frozen in a sealed container for use another time.

For the duck, prick the skin all over with a fork, and then crush the juniper berries, peppercorns, bay leaf with a pestle and mortar (or equivalent). Add the salt and garlic to the mix before marinating/seasoning the duck in a bowl. Cover with cling film, refrigerate, and leave for at least 2 hours (better still, overnight). Take the duck out of the fridge, and allow 30 minutes for it to reach room temperature.

Preheat the oven to 180°C (160°C fan) and scrape off the spice mix off the duck. Roast uncovered for 90 minutes, and then rest for 10 minutes under foil before shredding the duck with two forks.

To prepare the pizza, place the grill rack on its highest shelf in the oven, leaving room to fit a wide, heavy frying pan and turn the grill to its highest setting. Place the pan in the oven. Cut the tip off the fig, and slice into 6 good-sized chunks. Once hot, place the frying pan on the hob and set to a medium heat (no oil). Place the dough ball onto a well-floured surface, and press and flatten it out with your fingers, starting from the centre up to about 1cm from the edge. Take the dough onto the back of your hands so it hangs on your knuckles and your fingertips won't poke a hole in the dough. Now gently stretch that section of dough by widening your hands apart slightly, then shuffle the disc round to repeat on the next section and continue until you have a 10-11 inch base. Be careful not to stretch too wide as it will tear. (If a small hole appears try to close the gap by pressing down to reseal it). Place the dough in the frying pan, and drizzle over the olive oil. Now scatter the duck, figs, brie, and thyme on top. Drizzle Balsamic vinegar onto the figs, followed by the honey. After 1-2 minutes, take the frying pan and place it under the grill. Once the crust then browns off after about 1-2 minutes, you are ready to go.

PIZZA LOCO

PANCETTA, PICKLED DAMSONS AND CREAMY GOATS CURD PIZZA

THIS RECIPE IS INSPIRED BY MY FAMILY'S TRADITIONAL WEEKEND FRY UP WITH A DOLLOP OF PICKLED DAMSONS TO DIP YOUR BACON IN. THE RECIPE FOR THE DAMSONS COMES FROM AN ANCIENT WI RECIPE BOOK PASSED DOWN FROM MY GREAT GRANDMOTHER, AND THERE'S A REASON WHY WE HAVEN'T CHANGED ANYTHING IN ALL THESE YEARS – THE TASTE. MAKES 1

1 dough ball, left to prove for 1-2 hours

Flour, for dusting

1 dessertspoon extra virgin olive oil

60g fior di latte mozzarella, torn

2 dessertspoons goats curd (chevre if you can't get hold of curd)

4 slices pancetta

2 dessertspoons pickled damsons, stones removed (use spiced plum chutney if your damsons aren't ready)

FOR THE PICKLED DAMSONS:

350ml cider/spiced vinegar

680g damsons

340g sugar

1 inch stick of cinnamon

¼ teaspoon cloves tied in muslin cloth

FOR THE DOUGH (MAKES 4 X 10 INCH BASES):

1g fresh yeast (0.6 active dry yeast)

300ml tepid water

1 dessertspoon extra virgin olive oil (optional)

500g '00' flour

15g sea salt

For the pickled damsons, pour vinegar over the damsons and leave overnight.

Boil all the ingredients in a pan for 20-30 minutes. Remove the cloves and cinnamon before putting the damsons into warm jars and seal (jam jars or Kilners are ideal). Leave for at least a fortnight before eating (it's worth the wait). Remove the stones before adding to pizza.

For the dough, stir the yeast into the water until dissolved, and add the olive oil. In a large (2 litre) mixing bowl, sift in the flour and add the salt. Combine the salt and flour with your fingertips before making a well in the centre. Fill the well with some of the liquid and, using a wooden spoon, begin stirring the walls of flour into the mixture so it thickens. As it thickens, gradually add the rest of the liquid, and continue mixing with the spoon for a minute or so. Now scrape the dough from the spoon back into the mixture, and swap over to working the dough using only your fingers (dough builds up on the palms very easily). Work for a good 10 minutes to mop up all the flour, so the dough is roughly combined. It might look a little lumpy at this point, but don't worry. Lightly oil a clean bowl then place the dough in it before covering with cling film, and rest for 1 hour.

Flour a wooden board or surface and lay out the dough. Gently make a rough rectangle shape. Fold the four corners into the centre, one after the other. Repeat once more. The dough should now be much smoother. Oil a bowl that is twice the volume of the dough, and place the ball of dough in smooth-side up before rubbing a little oil over the top. Cover with cling film, and leave at room temp for 16-18 hours (at least 10 hours). Allow 1-2 hours longer if it's colder than room temperature.

Cut dough into four equal pieces using a sharp knife, and repeat the folding method as before. Then shape into balls. At this point, the dough balls can be frozen in a sealed container for use another time.

To prepare the pizza, place the grill rack on its highest shelf in the oven, leaving room to fit a wide, heavy frying pan on, and set the grill to its highest setting. Once hot, place the frying pan on the hob and set to a medium heat (no oil). Place the dough ball onto a well-floured surface, and press and flatten it out with your fingers, starting from the centre up to about 1cm from the edge. Take the dough onto the back of your hands so it hangs on your knuckles and your fingertips won't poke a hole in the dough. Now gently stretch that section of dough by widening your hands apart slightly, and then shuffle the disc round to repeat on the next section and continue until you have a 10-11 inch base. Be careful not to stretch too wide as it will tear. (If a small hole does appear, you may be able to close the gap and press down to reseal it).

Drop the dough onto the hot pan, drizzle over the olive oil, then add the mozzarella along with 5 blobs of damsons, 5 blobs of curd spread evenly, and then add the pancetta. Cook for 2 minutes on the hob until the base browns off.

Now, transfer to the shelf under the grill for another 2 minutes. Eat. And be happy.

SMO·FO SMOKED FOOD
PINT OF HICKORY SMOKED PORK SCRATCHINGS

THE DISTINCTIVE SMO·FO LABEL IS POPPING UP ACROSS SHEFFIELD, FLYING OFF THE SHELVES OF LOCAL FOOD RETAILERS AND ADORNING THE BARS AT PUBS WHERE NOT ONLY IS THE BEER TAKEN SERIOUSLY BUT THE BAR SNACKS ARE TOO. SIMON BARNES, FOUNDER OF SMO·FO HAD ALWAYS HAD A KEEN INTEREST IN THE AGE-OLD TRADITIONS OF PRESERVING FOOD. HE'D OFTEN SMOKED HIS OWN FOODS AT HOME, PASSIONATE ABOUT THIS SIMPLE METHOD OF ADDING FLAVOUR AND SHELF-LIFE TO FOOD, WHICH HAS BEEN PRACTISED ACROSS THE WORLD FOR HUNDREDS OF YEARS. SITTING IN THE BEER GARDENS OF SHEFFIELD, TABLES FULL OF LOVINGLY PRODUCED CRAFT BEERS, HE REALISED THAT A PACKET OF CRISPS JUST WASN'T GOING TO CUT THE MUSTARD. WHAT WAS NEEDED WAS A RANGE OF SNACKS THAT WERE PRODUCED WITH EQUAL CARE AND QUALITY. IN THE SHEFFIELD/DERBYSHIRE BORDERS, HE SET ABOUT CREATING A RANGE OF SNACKS COMBINING TRADITIONAL SMOKING TECHNIQUES AND MODERN FLAVOURS.

Here is SMO·FO Smoked Food's quick method for smoking foods in your own back garden. You will need to prepare the pork skin 1-2 days in advance to make sure it is thoroughly dried out. Serves 4-6

PORK SCRATCHINGS:

1kg pork skin, cut into strips

A handful of sea salt

4 'off-the-shelf' pork stock cubes

A good pinch of white pepper

EQUIPMENT:

1 unused traditional metal bird feeder

A barbecue with a shelf and a lid

500g hickory wood shavings (available on line)

1 tea-light candle

Salt both sides of the pork skin and stand on a tray. Leave uncovered in a fridge for 1-2 days until the pork has dried out. Pat the pork off with a clean tea towel to remove the salt and place on a wire rack. Pack the hickory wood as tightly as possible into a traditional metal bird feeder, leaving the top off and the shavings sticking out the top.

Outside, place the bird feeder in the bottom of the barbecue, light the tea-light candle and place the candle just under the open lip of the feeder so the flame can heat the shavings and keep the wood alight. Eventually the wood should slowly burn with little or no flame. Put the wire rack of pork on the barbecue shelf above the smoker, away from any flame and close the lid, leaving it ajar for a little ventilation. The wood should smoke for around 2-3 hours. Take the smoked pork out.

Heat the oil for deep-frying in a deep-fryer or heavy-bottomed pan to 120°C. Deep-fry the pork skin for 10 minutes, then carefully remove it and drain on kitchen roll. Turn the heat of the oil up to 190°C and fry the strips again for a further 3 minutes. Grind the stock cubes into a powder and mix with the white pepper. Season the scratchings to taste with the mixture. Serve in a pint glass.

CAFÉ CEREZA

AS ITS VIBRANT PACKAGING AND AWARD-WINNING DESIGN BECOME FAMILIAR ACROSS THE COUNTRY, WE ASK WHAT IS BEHIND THE POWERFUL BRANDING THAT SETS YORKSHIRE'S CAFÉ CEREZA APART FROM AN ORDINARY CUP OF JOE.

The world of coffee is changing. Among the ubiquitous brown paper bags of coffee, something new and exciting has arrived in the form of coffee company Café Cereza. Founded in 2012, the company stands out from the crowd; its branding, which won a national Fresh Creative Design Award in 2013, is inspired by the roots of the coffee bean, back in its colourful home of El Salvador.

Café Cereza's motto is "coffee that makes you feel good" – and it does, for a whole host of reasons; from evocative packaging, which captures the relaxed Latin American vibe and a dedication to working directly with producers in El Salvador, to the incredible and distinct flavour of its finest Strictly High Grown Bourbon Arabica.

The company works directly with the family-run Monte Sion Estate in El Salvador and has nurtured a close relationship with them; it enables the producers to negotiate the best deal for their coffee and Café Cereza to buy the finest product. The quality of the gourmet standard coffee is second-to-none and the taste has been a big hit with customers across the UK.

As the beans are sourced directly, Café Cereza has complete control over the roasting and packing, which is done in the UK to guarantee freshness. When so much work has gone into the process of producing the very finest coffee, Café Cereza is determined to ensure that its customers experience the best cup of coffee possible. This comprehensive approach includes full marketing support and barista training for its retail partners.

The company has also introduced versatile dual-fuel Piaggio coffee vans to the UK, which have proved a hit with universities as well as independent traders.

Executed properly by a trained barista, a cup of Café Cereza coffee is something to be savoured. Try a cup and let it transport you to El Salvador where celebrating the 'good life' is practically the law of the land – stop, relax and enjoy. Pura vida!

Café Cereza™

Coffee that makes you feel good!

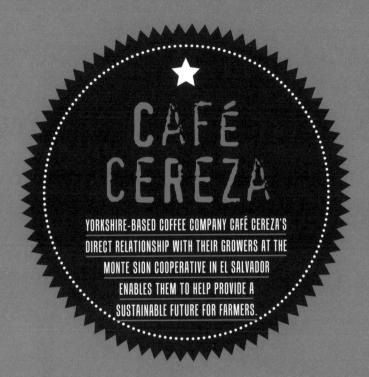

CAFÉ CEREZA

YORKSHIRE-BASED COFFEE COMPANY CAFÉ CEREZA'S DIRECT RELATIONSHIP WITH THEIR GROWERS AT THE MONTE SION COOPERATIVE IN EL SALVADOR ENABLES THEM TO HELP PROVIDE A SUSTAINABLE FUTURE FOR FARMERS.

While Monte Sion's rich, volcanic soil and perfect microclimate are two of the natural factors that make it an ideal area for farming coffee beans, nature can only provide so much. The rest of the work is undertaken by the dedicated, hard-working community of farmers and their families.

Monte Sion has been producing gourmet sustainable coffee since 1907 and is run by Lilliana de Narvaez and her father Dr. Luis Urrutia, who has been recognised by the UN for helping to combat poverty in El Salvador.

The quality of the coffee is underlined by a variety of accreditations; it has been certified by the Rainforest Alliance since 2000 and is a member of the Association of Sustainable Coffees of El Salvador.

Supporting producers has always been fundamental to Café Cereza's business practices. Bryan Unkles, the company's founder and director, has visited Monte Sion twice during the last five years and it is a place very close to his heart.

Lilliana and Luis have set up their own foundation – Fundacion Monte Sion Nuevo Amanecer – to which Café Cereza donates a percentage of its turnover. Funds from the foundation support workers and families by providing healthcare, housing, education, food and clothing.

Focusing on sustainability has helped provide a secure future for the people who farm Café Cereza coffee, but direct sourcing also has benefits for Café Cereza customers as it ensures consistency as well as a great choice of the very finest coffees.

The relationship between these two independent businesses, which work together across the globe, has provided significant benefits for each party. Café Cereza is a shining example of how successful partnerships can have positive effects for business, the environment and communities in two diverse countries, as well as ensuring its customers get to enjoy the ultimate Latin American beverage – "coffee that makes you feel good!"

DONT MAKE

WWW.BOST

IT WE'LL SHAKE IT

ONSHAKERS.CO.UK

BOSTON SHAKERS

PROFESSIONAL MIXOLOGISTS AND BESPOKE COCKTAIL SPECIALISTS BOSTON SHAKERS ARE TRAVELLING THE COUNTRY WITH THEIR MOBILE COCKTAIL BAR.

The glitz and glamour of a cocktail bar is irresistible. Myriad colours, dazzling decorations and astonishing glasses all combine to create an experience like no other. After years working as a bartender, learning the skills of mixology and professional cocktail-making, Metz Patel found that his natural charisma and creative flair behind the bar were setting him apart from other staff. Returning customers would request him by name and he was becoming the go-to mixologist for special events and private parties.

In 2013, Metz and two other bartenders decided to explore a gap in the market for mobile cocktails. At this point, Metz was working at the same time as doing his degree, balancing his university studies with developing the business idea. In 2014, he took the brave step to take a year away from his studies, buy out his partners and take his business forward into a full-time venture.

Festivals, weddings, private parties – bookings came in thick and fast for his unique approach to mobile catering. The focus is on creating an exciting atmosphere and giving people the freedom to select how they want their event to feel. Choose the style of bar, the variety of drinks and the type of hire you would like, and Boston Shakers will work with you to make sure you get the bespoke service that is perfect for your event.

Fancy something non-alcoholic? Don't worry, the professional mixologists have plenty of mouth-watering ideas for mocktails, too. They can even offer masterclasses to show us all a thing or two about making our own cocktails at home – perfect for hen parties, birthdays, corporate events and team-building days… or just for when you want to do something different with your friends.

After an incredibly successful 2015, and with an endless supply of ingredients, glassware, skill and creativity at their disposal, Boston Shakers are all set to continue shaking things up in 2016!

Espresso Martini

The Boston Shaker

Rum Old-Fashioned

BOSTON SHAKERS

COCKTAIL SELECTION

THREE IMPRESSIVE COCKTAILS, INCLUDING THEIR CLASSIC BOSTON SHAKER.

EACH SERVES 1.

RUM OLD-FASHIONED:

50ml Diplomatico Reserva Exclusiva

3ml Angostura bitters

3ml Orange bitters

Orange zest

3g caster sugar

Orange zest, to garnish

THE BOSTON SHAKER:

37.5ml Malibu

12.5ml Triple Sec

12.5ml fresh lime juice

12.5ml passion fruit purée

25ml apple juice

50ml pineapple juice

Dash of Grenadine

Pineapple wedge and pineapple leaves, to garnish

ESPRESSO MARTINI:

37.5ml Belvedere vodka

12.5ml Kahlua

12.5ml vanilla monin syrup

12.5ml sugar syrup

50ml fresh espresso

3 coffee beans, to garnish

RUM OLD-FASHIONED:

Take a peel of an orange and squeeze it with your fingers. Rub the peel around the insides of a old fashioned glass, then place into the glass. Add the caster sugar, orange and Angostura bitters into the glass and muddle.

Add four ice cubes and half of Diplomatico Reserva Exclusiva and stir for no less than ten seconds. Add more ice to fill and the remaining liquor and stir again for a further 10-15 seconds.

To serve, garnish with orange zest.

THE BOSTON SHAKER:

Take the mixing glass and fill with cubed ice. Add Malibu, Triple Sec, fresh lime juice, passion fruit purée, apple and pineapple juice to the glass and shake.

Add cubed ice to the sling glass and strain all the contents from the shaker.

To serve, add a dash of Grenadine into the sling glass and garnish with a pineapple wedge and pineapple leaves.

ESPRESSO MARTINI:

Chill a martini glass with ice and put to the side.

In the mixing glass, add the Belvedere, Kahlua, Vanilla Monin, fresh expresso and sugar syrup. Fill with cubed ice and shake vigorously, until the shaker is frosted.

Remove the ice from the Martini glass and fine strain in all the contents from the shaker.

To serve, garnish with 3 coffee beans.

THE DIRECTORY

BOSTON SHAKERS

Mobile cocktail bar offering a bespoke service

Telephone: 07718 081943

Website: www.bostonshakers.co.uk

Facebook: www.facebook.com/bostonshakers

Twitter: @bostonshakers

BUDDHA BELLY

Thai street food from MasterChef 2012 contestant.

Telephone: 07990 994078

Website: www.buddhabellystreetfood.co.uk

Facebook: www.facebook.com/saibuddhabelly

Twitter: @saibuddhabelly

CAFÉ CEREZA

A new coffee brand brought to you by Cafeology – coffee that makes you feel good.

Website: www.cafecereza.co.uk

Twitter: @CafeCerezaTime

Facebook: www.facebook.com/CafeCerezaTime

CRÊPE LUCETTE

Unique vintage crêpe experience.

Telephone: 07757 936652

Website: www.crepelucette.com

Facebook: www.facebook.com/crepelucette

Twitter: @crepelucette

FANCY AN INDIAN

Indian Street food from the 'wrapmobile', supper clubs and cooking classes in your own home.

Website: www.fancy-an-indian.com

Twitter: @_fancy_an_indian

Facebook: www.facebook.com/fancyanindian?

GINGER BAKERS

Hand-made cakes and bakes. Quality ingredients baked with care and generosity.

Telephone: 01539 422 084

Website: www.gingerbakers.co.uk

Twitter: @GingerBakers

THE HOG STOP

Slow-roasted pork sandwiches with international flavour combinations.

Website: www.thehogstop.co.uk

Telephone: 07789 775332

Email: info@thehogstop.co.uk

KHOO'S HOT SAUCE

Artisan chilli sauce made in Sheffield.

Website: www.khooshothouse.wordpress.com

Facebook: www.facebook.com/khooshotsauce

KITSCH'N CRÊPE CO.

Mobile crêpe company based in the North-east.

Telephone: 07939 575661

Website: www.kitschncatering.com

Facebook: www.facebook.com/kitschncrepeco

Twitter: @kitschncrepeco